...D STORIES

STEPS AND STORIES

History, Steps, and Spirituality of
Alcoholics Anonymous

Change Your Perspective,
Change Your Mind, Change Your World

by Sandy Beach

HOTCHKISS PUBLISHING

Library of Congress Control Number: 2015941458

ISBN 978-0-9909020-1-0 Paperback
ISBN 978-0-9909020-2-7 Hardbound

Edited by:
Allison Hagen, William J. Ludwig, Frederic G. Ludwig Jr.

Cover & Interior Design:
Karin Badger

First Edition: July 2015
Printed in the United States of America

Published by
HOTCHKISS PUBLISHING
17 Frank Street
Branford, CT 06405
info@HotchkissPublishing.com
www.HotchkissPublishing.com
www.Steps&Stories.com

Steps & Stories is dedicated to the loving memory of:
Barbara Beach Hamburg
Catherine Beach Barrett

Contents

Preface

FOR 18 YEARS Sandy presented a "lecture" style meeting, Saturday Morning Live, every weekend while he was living and working in the Washington, DC area. The meetings were held at Bethesda Hospital and later on, when a larger auditorium was needed, it moved to the National Institute of Health. For the first eight years he would talk about three of the twelve steps each week. The format then changed to one step each week for twelve weeks followed by one week on the Traditions and then two weeks on the history of Alcoholics Anonymous.

After retiring to Tampa, FL in 1996 he was asked to repeat this series on occasion. One of the first times he agreed to do this he ran through all the Steps and some history over the course of just one weekend. He was very happy with the result but said that it was exhausting. In 2007, Sandy combined the History, the Traditions, and the Steps in to a talk, which is the basis for this book. He titled the series Steps & Stories and it took place during twelve consecutive Sunday meetings at the Palma Ceia Presbyterian Church in Tampa. Recording for Lee's Tapes was deftly handled by Chris B., a sponsee and protégé of Sandy's. (To purchase CD's of the talks contact Lee's Tapes)

Hotchkiss Publishing has transcribed all 12 of the audio files in order to bring this important and helpful series to a wider audience.

It has become increasing popular to create audio versions of books. Audio is great but you cannot underline or highlight important passages you may want to come back to at a later date. Since Sandy's talks, until now, have only been available on tape, CD, or online audio we believe that many people would benefit from having a copy in print to read and to refer to now and over the years. The challenge of transcribing from audio to print has been to remove some of the "filler" phrases i.e. "do your follow what I am saying" or "do you know what I mean", and other speaking mannerisms and yet retain the speakers' "voice" and most importantly the speaker's message.

Since the talks were weekly, each would open with similar introductory remarks. Rather than repeat them in each chapter they have been consolidated and are presented in the front matter as Sandy's Introduction. We also tried to limit other such repeated material to streamline the text for better engagement with the reader. A few passages may seem awkward to those not too familiar with AA or Sandy's manner of speech, but we have elected to leave as much as possible true to his original manner of delivery.

Sandy's talks and recordings have helped many over the years more fully connect with the AA program and a spiritual way of life. It is our hope that this volume will continue that legacy by bringing his humble wisdom and humor to people who are new to sobriety and to those who have been around a while but are searching for a new perspective.

We have tried to fact check many of the references in the talk and have added a few corrections and/or additional details for clarity, which we hope the reader will find helpful.

Sandy's Introduction

"I WANT TO start out with sort of a disclaimer telling you what this is not. This is not a class on the steps or a workshop on the steps or once you've been here you don't need to talk to your sponsor anymore or anything like that. This is not a workshop or a Joe and Charlie or how to do the twelve steps of AA. I've been around a long time and I know a lot of stories—and I'm going to tell them all during these twelve chapters. In here you'll read about the steps, my thoughts about what the steps mean spiritually. And you'll read about AA and all of our comings and goings.

I hope through this that your perspective on AA will change. Now if you're new, I hope that you will hear things that make you very excited about being a member of AA and to realize how wonderful it really is. However, if I make some comment about one of the steps or a principle of the program and your sponsor has told you something else, pay attention to your sponsor. That's the person who is taking you through the steps, and that's who you want to follow. You want to follow that guidance!

I say that because everyone who has been around awhile sees it a little bit differently than the next person. There's no official version of anything, anywhere. What we have is the official literature, and *that* we stick with: the Big Book and the Twelve and Twelve. I am a great believer in both books. I know that the Twelve and

Twelve came in 1950, and the people who were around before felt like they didn't need any new guys on the block. But it was written by the same author, with twelve or fifteen years more sobriety. His perspectives, especially on about half of the steps, in the Twelve and Twelve, are just brilliant, absolutely brilliant. I mean, you look at Steps Six and Seven coming out of the Big Book, and we barely have a handle on them. Then here's the Twelve and Twelve; here's this wonderful explanation and portrait of them. I'm a believer in using both the books."

Editor's note: Sandy made these and similar remarks at the start of each week's talk. We offer here a combined version just this once to begin.

1

Four Thousand Years of Desperation

EVERY YEAR AROUND the anniversary of Alcoholics Anonymous, June 10th, ten thousand people descend on Akron, Ohio, completely overpowering the city's traffic as they run around, jumping up and down, celebrating not drinking. Now, AA has been hosting Founders' Day in Akron for a long time, so the residents are used to it. As a matter of fact, I was there last year; they plan their yard sales for when AA shows up, if you can imagine that.

You look around and you go, *Look at all the yard sales that are going on*. And then you find out, yeah, here are the most potential buyers that are ever wandering the streets, and they probably get a much better price. AA will be 72 years old [*80 in 2015 –Ed.*], and when I was born, there was no AA. Now think about that. Just in my lifetime, we've gone from nothing in the world that could help alcoholics to an organization that can boost the yard sale economy of an American town.

I learned a couple weeks ago from the General Service Manager from the New York office that "We've now translated all of our literature into 59 languages, and we're in 198 countries." That's pretty powerful stuff for the Big Book and the Twelve and Twelve. Those two books contain a way of life that, when alcoholics get a hold of it, gets them sober and happy. No matter where they live, no matter what they're drinking. That's pretty good evidence that this works.

If you go back to the beginning of recorded history, maybe 4,000 years ago, there's always mention of the alcoholics. We've been around forever. As soon as they fermented some wine, we found out how to drink it differently than everyone else and soon became the outcasts of society, whatever society it was. For all those years, the treatment of alcoholics was to ostracize them, to push them into a separate place, whether it was an institution, a jail or just out of town. Nothing was able to lay a glove on the disease of alcoholism. Not medicine, psychiatry, not anything … with two exceptions.

One of them came a hundred years before AA. Way back in the 1840s—and this is all true history. For those who haven't heard this story, five guys were drinking in a bar in Baltimore, and they were successful businessmen, middle-aged, and they knew that they had a drinking problem. They knew, as they discussed it amongst themselves, that they were going to lose their families, their businesses, the respect of the community, and they just pretty much accepted it.

They just said, "Well, let's enjoy it while we got it," because they could see the handwriting on the wall.

One of them said, "I wonder if we could keep each other sober?" And they all laughed at that and had another drink. And the man repeated, "No, I'm serious. We know we can't stay sober ourselves, but maybe we could keep each other sober. I'm going to go home and I'm going to write a pledge, a solemn pledge. Then we'll come back next week, and we'll all take the pledge together, in front of each other. Yeah, I'll drink to the pledge."

They came back the following week, and he had written out the pledge. It reads:

"We, whose names are annexed, desirous of forming a society for our mutual benefit and to guard against a pernicious practice which is injurious to our health, standing, and families, do pledge ourselves, as gentlemen, that we will not drink any spirituous or malt liquors, wine or cider."

They read it and solemnly took it with one another and went

home and didn't drink. They checked with each other each day, and pretty soon they had made it a week. They started telling other people in the city, *Why don't you come and stand in front of us and take the pledge?* So they did.

They were fairly well known businessmen, and they capitalized on this fact to attract others. Eventually they got the mayor. People sat around and thought, "Wow, the mayor just took that pledge. I ought to join that organization and get to hang around with the mayor." They kept doing this, and at the end of the first year, they had 4,000 people in a parade. Four thousand people!

They decided it was so amazing that they should spread it around the rest of the United States. They assigned vice presidents to go to other cities, such as Philadelphia, New York, and Washington, D.C. And they took the pledge and the message up to these other cities. At the end of four years, they had around 300,000 people who had taken the pledge and were part of this thing that started in Baltimore, Maryland. Now 300,000 people, at the end of four years is a lot of people. AA claimed one hundred members, but we know they only had about seventy. We exaggerated even back then.

Now once this thing got successful, they were sitting around, the original five guys, and they said, *We have to name this. Why don't we name it after the number one man in America, George Washington? That'll get even more attention.* So they named it The Washingtonian Society, and it never had anything more than the pledge. It was kind of like a pyramid scheme, where the excitement was bringing in more people to the parade and then asking them, "How about you take the pledge?" Now that it was successful like that, with high publicity, it was in the papers; Abraham Lincoln gave a speech at one of their annual conventions. (This was before he was president, but he was one of the people who spoke to them about the wonderful work they were doing.)

About that time the country was very interested in the Temperance Movement. The Temperance forces thought The

Washingtonian Society would be a great group to endorse Prohibition. The movement to end slavery was picking up momentum, too. They thought that this movement with all these sober people would be a wonderful shot in the arm for the abolition movement. That's a wonderful cause to get involved in. They got involved with both of those causes, which we now know as "outside issues," when you look at our Traditions.

Within a year, no one was left sober or in the organization. It disappeared off the face of this country to such an extent that, in the late 1940s, when Bill Wilson was writing The Traditions, he had never heard of them. He was writing about how the organization should handle the problems it was encountering as it got bigger, and one of Bill's friends said, *You ought to look at The Washingtonian Society and get some ideas from them.* He had never heard of them. How about that? He had never heard of them.

When you disappear, you disappear. So for that little period, there was a little glimmer of hope for alcoholics, and then that disappeared. My point in telling these stories about the history is to begin to establish how powerful the disease of alcoholism is. That throughout recorded history; nothing was able to do anything, really, about it, until 1935 when Bill Wilson and Dr. Bob Smith, in a chance meeting, began this thing that we know as Alcoholics Anonymous.

Now another historical precedent about the powerlessness we have—because that's really what our first step is all about—is in the early history of AA itself. Some of you may not have heard the origins of how Bill got sober, so I'll tell you briefly. In the late 1920s, there was a millionaire who belonged to a very wealthy family in Rhode Island named Rowland Hazard. A lot of people still know the Hazard name up in Rhode Island. He was to take over the family business, but he was an alcoholic, and it became obvious that he was not going to last. He himself realized that. He had been hospitalized and hospitalized, and out of desperation, because they had unlimited money, they decided to send him to

Switzerland to see a psychiatrist named Dr. Carl Jung. He stayed with that psychiatrist for a year and saw him every week, and Dr. Jung attempted in those therapy sessions to cause Hazard to have a profound personality change, so that he would look at the world differently and wouldn't have to drink.

At the end of the year, Jung said to Rowland, *You understand your situation. You understand that if you do go back to drinking, it's very likely you'll end up in a sanitarium somewhere. So good luck and just stay away from the alcohol.* He thanked Dr. Jung and left Switzerland. On his way back to the United States, he went through Paris.

Somebody in Paris asked him the wrong question. They said, *Would you like a drink, Rowland?* and he said, *Don't mind if I do.*

And in a matter of a few months, he was back to see Dr. Jung, in worse shape than he was when he got there the first time. He came back and he said, *Dr. Jung, you've got to help me. Now I'm worse off than I was. Please, please help me.*

Dr. Jung looked at Rowland and said something that started Alcoholics Anonymous: *There's nothing I can do for you.* Now that'll pull the rug out from under you! *I'm sorry, son, there's nothing I can do for you.* That was a great act of humility, when you're one of the smartest psychiatrists on the planet and you're willing to admit there's nothing you can do.

Rowland said, *Nothing?*

Jung said, *No, I can't. I tried. I did everything that I know how to do, and it didn't work.* What he induced with that statement in Rowland was an absolute state of desperation. The state that we all encountered. Absolute hopelessness. Then he said, *Now I have heard of a few cases where people found a spiritual way to have a profound change. If I were you, I would go try to find that.*

He didn't even tell him where to look. Now I submit to you, had Jung said those two things in the reverse order, if he had simply suggested a spiritual approach, Rowland never would have gone. Jung first had to tell him, *There's nothing I can do for you.*

Bill Wilson later wrote a letter to Dr. Jung to thank him for helping to start Alcoholics Anonymous.

Whenever I see that sentence, I think of the beginning of chapter five that we read at the AA meetings, with the ABCs at the end. Three pertinent ideas:

The first one, which we've been talking about, is that **we're powerless over alcohol.**

The second one is that **no human power could have relieved our alcoholism.** I picture Dr. Jung looking at Rowland—I mean, this is the end of the human power—and saying, *There's nothing I can do for you.* The third is that **God could and would if he were sought.** And that's what we all have to come to grips with, in one way or another, in our own lives, is the realization that there isn't anything on the planet that can help us, other than spirituality. Whoa!

That's where it started. At that time there was a spiritual movement in the 1920's that had started with a Lutheran minister who got tired of the bureaucracy and the hierarchy of the church. He said, *The problem with religion is the middleman. These churches and all these people in the middle. We ought to just meet in small groups and talk about spirituality among ourselves, and that's how we'll get spiritual. We'll leave out the churches.*

It caught on. His name was Frank Buchman, and it was called the Oxford Movement. After Buchman had spread it across the United States and England, he traveled to South Africa with a group from Oxford University. The South Africans would say, *Those guys from Oxford are here*, and the name stuck. It was very big at that time in the United States.

Rowland came back from Switzerland and joined an Oxford Group. He got sober and stayed sober for a number of years. It's unclear whether he died sober, because he did not become a member of AA after AA got started. But he was the messenger for all of us in this room that started the whole thing. He had a summer home in Manchester, Vermont. This became a very crucial city in the history of AA, because Bill Wilson was born about five miles from Manchester. He went to Burr and Burton Academy in Manchester.

Dr. Clark Burnham, from Brooklyn, also had a summer home in Manchester. Dr. Burnham's daughter was Lois Burnham, who later became the founder of Al-Anon and the wife of Bill Wilson. And that's where they met, in Vermont. Over from Albany, New York, where his father was the mayor, was Ebby Thacher. Thacher is a big name up in Albany. I think there's a Thacher Park and a Thacher Square, and they had a summer home there, as well.

Ebby was a raging alcoholic and a big friend of Bill Wilson's. And they did a lot of drinking together and partying. Ebby was on his way to his bottom, even driving a car into a farmhouse on a Saturday morning, drunk. He went all the way through the living room to the kitchen, at which point he asked the farmer's wife for a cup of coffee. So we were spectacular alcoholics back in the '30s. Ebby went in front of the judge, and the judge let him go and said, *Look, you've got to behave yourself. We all know you—you've got a good family, so please try harder.* He tried harder.

His family made a deal with him. They said, *Ebby, you know the summer home in Manchester? If you agree to stay there and never come to Albany, where you are embarrassing us*—because his father was thinking of running for vice president and he didn't need Ebby creating sensational stories to ruin his campaign—*we'll give you the home and an allowance.*

He said OK.

So he had his drinking money, he had a home—couldn't have a better deal than that. One day he was quite drunk and he decided that the house needed painting. He said, *I'm going to paint my house.* How many alcoholics have done that? *I'm going to paint this house.* We go downtown and we buy a couple bottles of booze, a ladder, some paint, and a paintbrush and come home and have a few drinks. Then we actually get the paintbrush out, paint maybe fifteen, twenty square feet, then we go over, sit down, and have a drink. We kind of look at the nice job we've done and imagine the whole house painted. You ever do that? *Man, this is really going to look good.*

And he was watching the paint dry when some birds came by and crapped all over the fresh paint, and they got him furious. He went inside and got a couple of shotguns, sat out there with his alcohol, and any bird that came anywhere near his yard—*bam!* He was firing the shotguns, and the neighbors were getting quite upset. They called the sheriff, and Ebby was arrested for firing guns and scaring people.

He was in front of the judge, and the judge was thinking of sending him to jail when Rowland Hazard came in. Rowland asked the judge if he would please release Ebby to his care. He said, *I'll be responsible for him.* Well, with that family name and all of that, the judge felt comfortable sending him off with Rowland. Rowland took him to the Oxford Movement and Ebby got sober.

They both went down to New York City to help the Oxford Group with soup kitchens and other charitable efforts. And while he was there, Ebby got to thinking about his drinking buddy, Bill Wilson, whom he knew was in New York, in Brooklyn. Out of the blue he called him up to see how he was doing. Bill Wilson, our co-founder, was on his last legs. He had been very successful on Wall Street but had lost everything. Nobody would hire him. His wife was working in a department store, and he was stealing money from her purse in order to buy gin. He thought that he could put together a great big deal so they would be rich again, but it was an illusion. He'd been through a local hospital a couple of times where our dear AA friend, Dr. Silkworth, had been working with him.

Ebby called him up and wanted to know how he was doing. Bill invited him over. It was Saturday, Lois had gone to work, he had a bottle of gin, and he could hardly wait. He thought the two of them would sit there and reminisce. When Ebby showed up, Bill looked at him—he looked healthy, and that scared Bill.

He said, *Ebby, what's wrong? You look healthy.*

Ebby said, *Bill, I found religion.*

Don't worry, we can rid you of that. Come on in, come on in. I've got a bottle of gin—we can get drinking again.

No, Bill. I found this thing—this Oxford thing. I've never been so happy.

Bill looked at him, and he *did* look really happy. He couldn't figure it out. Bill went to church, he tried to believe in God, but he just couldn't believe in the divinity of anything. He sat there looking at Ebby and he couldn't deny that Ebby looked wonderful. And he started talking to Ebby about his problems believing in God and church and all the things he had when he was a little kid.

Ebby looked at him and said, *Well, Bill, why don't you choose your own conception of God?* There was no way that Bill could argue with that. How are you going to argue with that? He thought about it and thought about it. But he drank the bottle and drank another one and ended up back in the hospital. He had never felt so depressed. He was down, just on his last legs.

Out of desperation, he thought about what Ebby said. Bill figured, *I might as well give it a try.* He said, *God, if there is a God, please show yourself to me.* The room lit up. There was a bright light, he recalled, a wind, sort of like being on a mountaintop. There were a couple of minutes of just wind noise and bright light, but as it was happening, he could feel the desire to drink leaving him. And he sat there just astounded at the end of that experience.

Now we have another psychiatrist who saved us, and that's Dr. Silkworth. A little while later, Dr. Silkworth came in to see how Bill was doing, and Bill said, *Doctor, you're not going to believe what just happened. Right in this room, there was this bright light. God came into this very room, and the wind was blowing, and I saw all these wonderful things, and I don't feel like drinking.*

Now, I can imagine a few psychiatrists who would say, *Oh, very interesting. Why don't you take some of these pills and calm down?*

But Dr. Silkworth said, *If I were you, I would believe that and I would go with it.* That was just wonderful! *If I were you, I would believe that and go with it.* He did and he went over to find Ebby at the Oxford Group. Bill had previously gone drunk a couple times to the Oxford Group meetings, but now he got sober, never took another drink, and never had a desire to drink—even though he had the worst time in those early years, always being broke, just one failure after another.

But that was the beginning of you and me sitting in this room. Then he went on to talk to Dr. Bob out in Akron. I'm not going to go through all that part of it, but out of all of that turmoil came the fellowship of Alcoholics Anonymous. They borrowed the principles of the Oxford Movement and turned them into the Twelve Steps that we are living by today. Eventually the alcoholics separated from the Oxford Movement, and we came up with the title for our book *Alcoholics Anonymous*, which was the title Bill wanted. Now the majority, as I understand it, wanted *The Way Out*. Bill didn't like that. He went to the Library of Congress, and there were ten other books called *The Way Out*. He knew the drunks wouldn't want to be number eleven in anything, and there was no book called *Alcoholics Anonymous*. So playing to their egos, it was real easy to get the book named *Alcoholics Anonymous*. (I'm wandering all over on historical stuff, 'cause I like it.)

In the beginning there were so few alcoholics in the little cities where it got started that they were afraid that, if it were publicly known, the number of drunks wanting to get sober would be overpowering. They assumed there would be people knocking on the door demanding entry, such was the power of the egos then. *If they find out we have this organization, there'll be thousands of them waiting in line to get into AA, and it'll drive us crazy. We won't be able to handle them all so we have to stay anonymous.*

In other words, the reason for anonymity was quite different than it is now. They adopted that, and then as time went on, they found the great spiritual value of anonymity and maintaining it at the level of press, radio, and films. Not breaking the anonymity of new people, not promoting Alcoholics Anonymous at all, but relying on other people to promote it for us, like reporters and doctors. It's worked all these years. It's a program of attraction, not promotion.

Bill took the six principles of the Oxford Group and was in the process of working on the book. People were pressuring him to get more done. They had farmed out the stories for the members to write for the back of the book. The members that didn't know how to write very well had some reporters helping them with their stories, so God knows whether they got edited or whatever. But we did end up with some wonderful stories. And Bill was writing and writing and he was postponing the chapter "How It Works." He was dreading finally getting down to the nuts and bolts of How it Works, because there were so many different ways that people talked about how it worked. In New York City it was kind of an agnostic, atheist crowd, who thought it ought to be a psychological program. They had their voices going, *Blah, blah, blah, enough of this God stuff. It's this thing, you get in here and you just...*

And then out in Akron, they said, *Look it has to be Jesus, or we're not going.* We had the Jesus crowd and the agnostic crowd coming to grips with each other and out of that helter-skelter came *God as we understand Him.* Bill doesn't give the credit to Ebby on that one; he says it was out of this clashing of ideas and compromises. Then going from the six principles to the Twelve Steps, Bill sat in his bed trying to come up with the final version to submit to the fellowship, and he knew he was going to hear all kinds of arguing back and forth. He sat there going, *The drunks are wiggling through some of the loopholes of these six principles. I'm going to write some loophole closers to fill in between these things.*

He started inserting what he called *loophole closers,* and when he got finished closing the loopholes, he looked down, and he had twelve. He felt twelve was such a wonderful number. He said, *Oh, twelve, twelve is so cool. It's very biblical, we've got twelve months, I like twelve.* We ended up with these Twelve Steps and later on the Twelve Traditions, and as these Twelve Steps are incorporated into the alcoholic's life, miracles take place on a routine basis. Absolutely routine. They happen so routinely we don't even label them miracles anymore. *Oh yeah, his family is back together. He's a productive member of society. He's going to work and supporting things and he's helping out everywhere. He used to be a selfish, self-centered bum who wouldn't do anything for anybody.*

And we forget that that is a miracle. To transform that individual from this to that. And that's what happened with our Twelve Steps. And in the foreword to the Twelve and Twelve, Bill describes what he thinks the Twelve Steps are. It's a two-sentence thing that says, "AA's Twelve Steps are a group of principles, spiritual in nature, which if practiced as a way of life will accomplish two things: one, it will expel the obsession to drink; and two, it will enable the suffering alcoholic to become happily and usefully whole." There's the author's assessment of what these steps are. They will get rid of the obsession to drink and enable you to become happily and usefully whole; a complete person.

If I wanted to, I could go to our literature and I could show you where the second step appears in the Big Book, and you would notice—my God—it's way up around page 50. With all of the steps and the preface, with the Roman numerals, it is like sixty pages before we get to the second step. Why? Because the first step is that important, that's why! The first step says we are powerless over alcohol and our lives have become unmanageable. That's exactly what I've been talking about for forty minutes is the powerlessness that this disease inflicts on society and how, for 4,000 years, no one could lay a glove on the disease of alcoholism. If it hadn't been for a miraculous little series of events, alcoholics would still be committed to nut wards or just out on the street, outcasts from society, and we would not have two to three million miracles around the world. All of that came because of the power of these Twelve Steps.

But the problem is—the Twelve Steps, the other eleven steps, will never be attempted unless you have to. You just aren't going to talk anybody into making amends, a moral inventory, prayer, meditation, admitting when you're wrong—you're not going to talk them into that, unless they have to. So AA in no way tries to convince you of the existence of God, even though we talk about God all the time. There's no AA God. If there are 150 people here, there are 150 different Higher Powers. It's not a religion, so no one here is trying to convince you that there is a God.

But I'll tell you what we're good at. We're good at convincing you that you need to find a God or you're screwed. That's what we're good at.

Hey, I understand you're not interested in spirituality.

No, I'm not.

How about if I hold this .45 to your head…

Well, I'll try it now.

It's like Tony Soprano saying, *Why don't you get spiritual?*

Oh, OK, where's the prayer?

That's the first step. I'm simplifying it, but that's what it is. It is saying you are powerless and your life is unmanageable and there's no human power that can help you. So that's why we take a long time. You'll see in our literature, it suggests to you that people who have been sober for a number of years who aren't happy, who just aren't getting it, never took the first step 100 percent. They are almost as bad as the rest of us were at the beginning. They have a problem, but not the same problem that the rest of us have. It's a modified version of our problem. Slightly less serious, slightly different. Just a little bit different. A little bit different childhood, little different part of the country, little different background. Whatever. We're off in a little different part of AA.

When you start out with being *almost* powerless over alcohol and *almost* having an unmanageable life, then you *almost* need a sponsor and you *almost* really need to do these steps and you *almost* get sober. *Almost* getting sober is very much like almost having a parachute. After the plane gets blown up and you're out in the air, it's too late to say, *You know, I almost took a parachute before we came up here tonight.* Too late!

So what do we mean when we say *powerless?* Most newcomers

think this means that whenever they drink, they get all messed up. They think that alcohol being in their system causes all the problems. The problem with that limited definition of alcoholism is the following: You go to treatment, you learn all about alcoholism, and you say to yourself, *You know something? They're right. Holy cow, I am an alcoholic. If I drink, I'm going to die. I mean I believe that to my soul. I honestly understand, as I never understood before, that I'm an alcoholic and I should never, ever drink.*

That knowledge and that insight is useless. Now how do you like that? It will not keep us sober. Why? Because the disease of alcoholism is fatal because it gets us when we're sober. We are absolutely powerless over alcohol when we have no alcohol in our system. We have no defense against the first drink. That defense has to come from a Higher Power. An alcoholic who's learned this goes—*Oh my God, I'm so excited and I'm not drinking anymore.* Then comes the insanity of alcoholism. He goes back to his old bar where some of his friends hang out. He likes to eat there. They have the best sandwiches in the world, and he's sharing with the bartender.

Joe, you know I'm an alcoholic?

Well, I thought maybe you might be.

Well, I am. I found out. I went to treatment. I understand alcoholism. It's an allergy, an obsession, just—oh my God, I'm so glad to find this out. If I ever have another drink, my wife is leaving me. It's that simple. That's where it is. And the doctor said if I ever do any more damage to my liver … could I have a beer? If I ever do any more…

What was that? He just ordered a beer while he was explaining the fatal nature of his own situation. Does that sound crazy? Uh huh, that's us. Fully understanding that alcohol will kill us, we go order another drink and we tell ourselves this time it'll be different. This time it will be different. So we're stuck with a hopeless situation where we're damned if we do and damned if we don't. There's no way that you, as an alcoholic, aren't going to drink again, unless a miracle takes place. And so that puts us in a very tough situation.

We have to come to grips with the fact that there's no way we can stay sober without alcohol, but the alcoholic is facing what I saw as two horrible choices.

One, I keep drinking, and these horrible things keep getting worse.

OK, I don't want that choice, so what's my second choice?

Don't drink at all. Now there's a good one. *OK, I'm going to choose choice number two. I'm not going to drink at all.* You know what happens when you don't drink at all? You are sober all the time. All day, all night, all week, all month, all year. No break. There's no break ever from being sober. Well, I don't know about the rest of you, but that's why I drank. I needed a break from being sober. That's what alcoholism is—we can't stand being sober. Our lives are so painful and unmanageable that we need relief from them. I remember it.

Oh boy, three more hours, three more hours, three more hours.

No more of that. That's why when people said to me, *Just don't drink*, I went, *You're crazy. Why would I do that?* So do you see what has to happen in order for an alcoholic to survive? Something has to happen so they can not drink and be happy. That is the transforming miracle of our Twelve Steps. That is what happens. No alcoholic can just stay sober on willpower and be in pain for the next thirty years. You just can't do it, it's too hard.

We spent all this time setting up the first step, so that when you take it, you take it with absolute despair. *OK, holy cow, now we're willing to do the rest of the steps.* Finally we have this willingness and open-mindedness to do things that we think are stupid.

I read those steps, and I said, *Are you kidding? This is going to help me? I need money, man. I've got six kids, and I'm out of the Marine Corps. I need money. And this is all abstract—inventory, spirituality? Get out of here.* So what was going to motivate me to do those steps? The first step. So if you are new, that is the key to long-term sobriety—100 percent surrender, so that you are eagerly looking forward to solving this horrible situation that you're in. The point of the first step, to tell you quite frankly, is to convince you that your situation is a lot worse than you think it is. Now that's not good news, but it is good news because if you suddenly realize, *Oh my God, it is so bad, I might pray,* that's pretty bad. I mean it has to be bad to do that.

That's why we spend all this time setting up the powerlessness and the unmanageability. So that you won't walk away from the first step thinking that the rest of it is kind of optional. *Well, I'll work a few of the steps so when I go to meetings it'll sound like I know what I'm talking about.* I remember doing that. I had little underlines in the Big Book and I'd go, *What was that?* "Rarely have we seen a person…"—I used to say that. I know drunks like that and they *call* them "Rarely."

I hope you've gotten an idea of the magnitude of this program and what it took for the universe to give us a solution. Most of us realize that Bill Wilson did not know how to write a book like this. That there was inspiration coming in 1934 and 1935 that began this process, and that that inspiration is being passed on around the world today as that very simple message is handed to one alcoholic after another. The secret of AA is one drunk talking to another. There's nothing else. Everything else in AA is to facilitate one drunk talking to another. We have conventions, we have meetings, we have literature, we've got all of that, but the real action is the sponsor talking to the alcoholic.

Bill used to tell a story where somebody said, *My God, you're drunks. Nobody knows what's going on. It's the blind leading the blind,* and Bill said, *No, it's the semi-blind leading the blind.* Because there it was—we had people with three months' sobriety going to Chicago to start AA there. *Oh yeah, take a book and go find a drunk.* Chicago has great AA now, but that's what was happening. It was just one person showing another one what they had already done. So all the people here who have a good bit of time, men and women who sponsor people, they are the custodians of this message. If you're new, please learn the message as it is in the book so that you can pass it on to the next person—and you're going to be called on in your first year to pass this on to somebody newer than you. So please take the time to understand each of our steps the way they're written down, so that the message that you pass on to the next drunk will work. Their life will be transformed.

2

This Thing Called a Higher Power

THE TWELVE STEPS are best described in the foreword to the Twelve and Twelve by Bill when he called them "a group of principles, spiritual in nature, which if practiced as a way of life will do two things. They will get rid of the obsession with alcohol, and enable you to become happily and usefully whole."

Being a complete person and being a happy person is what the twelve principles are designed to give you. I have been saying this for 30 years. *If you're in Alcoholics Anonymous, have been in here a while, and you're working the steps and you are not happy, you are doing it wrong*, because they're designed to enable us to have an underlying sense of joy and happiness even when sad events are happening.

In other words, they co-exist. We always have that sense of optimism, even as we're going through losing a job, a relationship, parents, or whatever it is. There is that eternal sense that everything is fine in spite of any seeming evidence to the contrary.

That's what is in store for you. If you are new, I wish you the best of luck and I hope you get as excited and enthusiastic about it as a lot of us are, because it never wears off. I've been enthusiastic for forty-some years, and it just doesn't go away! It's here. It would go away if I stopped coming here and stopped being plugged into it, but I have no intention of doing that.

You may know my story. I was a Marine pilot, and the Navy was in charge of all of our medical needs. It was the dark ages as far as alcoholism was concerned. I just received a notice that a Navy doctor, Dr. Joe Zuska, passed away at age 93 [*in May 2007 –Ed.*].

He was a doctor in World War II—the Battle of Tarawa, the Battle of Saipan—and was on a hospital ship during the Inchon landings. He ended up in Long Beach in the '60s, and a retired Navy commander was visiting with him. His visitor was a recovered alcoholic in AA, and he asked him what the Navy was doing for alcoholics. Dr. Zuska said *nothing*.

The Navy policy at that time was that alcoholism was punishable by time in the brig. When Dr. Zuska saw what was going on (and the fact that the Navy at the same time encouraged a lot of drinking), he thought that something ought to be done. According to his LA Times obituary,

Though the program had not been approved by Navy officials, Zuska began holding weekly meetings of Alcoholics Anonymous in a conference room at the naval station, then moved to the Quonset hut when the number of participants grew. The doctor found an 80-bed barracks and turned it into an inpatient recovery facility. Word soon spread that lives were being changed, and higher-ups in the Navy found out.

"The brass was alarmed for two reasons: According to policy there were no alcoholics in the Navy at that time, hence there was no need for a treatment policy; and there were quite a few alcoholic admirals and generals on active duty in the Pentagon," (Dr. Joseph A.) Pursch wrote in a 1987 column for The Times.

A commission was sent to investigate what was called an illegal activity, but it acknowledged that the Navy had alcoholics and that the treatment program Zuska had created was effective.

In 1967 the Pentagon gave Zuska approval for the first official Alcohol Rehabilitation Center, and by 1971, 70% of 900 patient admissions showed "demonstrated improvement."[1]

I just wanted to mention that because it is hard to imagine that I was back there then and that the only thing available was the brig. You had to hide it, and when I did go in, I was sent into the nut ward, and AA found me.

In the last chapter, we discussed Bill's spiritual experience in Towns Hospital. In that experience, Bill had the desire to drink lifted out of him while he was in the hospital and barely sober, and he never drank again.

Out of that experience, called the spiritual awakening, came two things: one, the freedom from the obsession with alcohol, and two, an absolute necessity to pass this message on. He couldn't restrain himself. The transformation was so exciting that he just knew he had to give it away, which is part of our whole program.

So he went out immediately when he was released from the hospital to sober alcoholics up. He went around to the bars. What did he have to talk about? What he had to talk about was this huge spiritual awakening. Everywhere he went he talked about this big moment *and the lights and the mountaintop, and God was there*. You know, if you are in the bar talking to an alcoholic who is having a few drinks about the mountaintop and the lights and all that, you're really not going to get too many takers.

People would say, *Well, I get that when I drink rum. I'm very familiar with that experience.*

Try as he would, he couldn't get anybody interested in his great recovery, until he went back and talked to Dr. Silkworth, who was the doctor at Towns Hospital. Dr. Silkworth was a psychiatrist, who by accident got into the alcohol business. He was a very prosperous psychiatrist, but the Crash of 1929 put him out of business. Charles Towns who owned the Towns Hospital was not a doctor. He was an entrepreneur, and he hired Dr. Silkworth to work with alcoholics. Silkworth took the job because it was all that was available.

---

1. Stewart, Jocelyn Y., "Joseph Zuska, 93; Long Beach Navy doctor was a pioneer in treating alcoholism." LA Times, 24 May 2007. http://articles.latimes.com/2007/may/24/local/me-zuska24

But it's lucky he got there. He told Bill, *You know, I don't think that hot flash story is going to work. So, you have to talk about the dead-end nature of the disease. You have to tell them that if they keep drinking, they're going to just keep going down, down, down, and make it so awful that they're ready to surrender.*

You can see how our steps got put into sequence right there. Bill was starting with the twelfth step, spiritual awakening, and ended up putting that at the very end. He determined that the first step was the most important, because unless we can accept all the way down to our very core that we are powerless over alcohol and unless something spiritual helps us, we will never make it. Whatever bad things have happened so far, much worse things are going to happen in the future.

When we all arrive here, we go, *Oh, yeah, I got a drinking problem, but I'm not quite the same as some of these hopeless jerks. Mine is more situational. My boss was mean to me, and if you were married to the woman I'm married too, you would drink a lot too. But I'm getting a divorce. That's going to take the pressure off, so I won't be drinking this much.*

You understand how you talk yourself out of being an alcoholic of the "hopeless" variety, because the "hopeless" variety has to do the steps, and nobody wants to do the steps.

I want to be almost hopeless, so I'll just hit some meetings and go out to lunch. That ought to carry me.

And we find out it carries us to the grave, but we all go through the game of pretending that things aren't as bad as they are.

As a matter of fact, some of us arrived here and didn't even identify as alcoholics. We become alcoholics while attending meetings. How could that happen? You come here and you're not an alcoholic, and then you go to about twenty-five meetings and you go, *You know something? I am an alcoholic and have been one for twenty years.*

How could that happen? We got honest. We finally got honest with ourselves and we took a close look and we saw this was indeed a terrible situation.

I read a book where Dr. Jung, Rowland Hazard's psychiatrist, was quoted, and I had never seen this quote before. Someone asked him what the main purpose of religion was. He said, "The main purpose of religion is to prevent people from having direct contact with God themselves." You go to church, and the church has the contact. You chip the money in, and they'll take care of you, and the contact will occur later on. Later on, you will actually have contact.

Of course, that's the difference with AA—we are working on contact with our own creator, direct personal contact, as opposed to a lot of knowledge about the creator. AA doesn't have any of that knowledge. We just have twelve suggested principles that will establish your own contact, and you will have your own experience. That becomes the foundation of your life.

Anyway, Bill was about to go back to work, try to earn a living, and recoup from the terrible situation they were in. He was sent out—after about five months' sobriety—to Akron, Ohio, on what turned out to be a failed business trip, where we run into the second key player in our lives, Dr. Bob Smith. Oddly enough, he was also from Vermont.

Whenever I'm in California, I love to remind them that the greatest social movement on planet Earth didn't start in California. You know what I hear? They go, *Yeah but it was going nowhere until we got in. Then we really got it going.* In all fairness, they are really fired up out there. It just amuses me that of all the places, they were both from Vermont. You wouldn't ever put that in a Hollywood movie—"Let's have both guys come from Vermont"—but they did.

Now, Dr. Bob was sixteen years older than Bill. His father was a judge, and he grew up in St. Johnsbury, Vermont, further north from where Bill grew up. Dr. Bob was a good student and he went to Dartmouth College. While he was there, he learned about drinking. Dartmouth still has that wonderful reputation of party, party, party. But he graduated. He hadn't really picked up the pace to the point where it was screwing up his life yet. He decided to be a doctor and went to the University of Michigan Medical School, and he lasted about four months before he had to drop out. Due to drinking, he couldn't possibly keep up with his studies.

He went back to Vermont and took about four months off. Then he returned and registered at a different school, Rush Medical College. After about six months, his father came and got him and brought him back to Vermont. This became a pattern. His father would rescue him, take him back, and watch him so he couldn't drink, and then send him back into action.

He eventually graduated from medical school and was lucky to get an internship in Akron, Ohio. He started his practice, and for the first couple years, he really didn't drink that much. He got involved with his practice and was building it … but then he just lost total control and had to go back to Vermont again. Again, he stayed for about six months with his father, came back, stayed sober about a year, and then just started being terrible.

He was hospitalized probably three times as many times as Bill, but he wouldn't let it get so bad that he couldn't return to performing surgery. Bill would go all the way down until he was a babbling idiot on the floor and then go in just before he died. Whereas Dr. Bob was going more frequently, both were in really hopeless situations.

Right around 1931, a funny event happened with the Firestones. Everybody knows Firestone Tires and Harvey Firestone, the multimillionaire. A gentleman from Fort Myers, Florida arrived in Akron to be a special secretary to Harvey Firestone. He was a member of the Oxford Group, and he noticed that Firestone's son Bud was an alcoholic. He was just drunk all the time.

So, he talked to Bud and he said, *You know, I'm in this Oxford Group, and I've seen alcoholics get sober in Oxford.* (Bill Wilson and Ebby Thacher were two of them.) He said, *Why don't you come with me to an Oxford Group meeting and see if you like it?* He went to this meeting out of state, and when they came back, Bud stayed sober. Bud Firestone stayed sober.

After a couple of years, his father said, *Well, we ought to get that Oxford crowd here in Akron*. The Oxford Group liked celebrities. They liked the whole idea that celebrities would attract more people to come into the movement. With Harvey Firestone, it was a big public relations deal. It was the social event of the year. *The Oxford people are coming!* Even Sam Shoemaker came. They took over the Mayflower Hotel and they had a huge deal.

Because of all that publicity, Dr. Bob's wife, Anne Smith, and Henrietta Seiberling, who become important players in our history, went to see what it was all about, and they liked it. They started attending. It was very beneficial to their lives, and they had quite a solid group there in Akron. After a year or so, Anne Smith said to her husband, *You ought to come with me to these Oxford Group meetings. We meet up once a week—they have had success with alcoholics, and I think it would help you.*

So, Dr. Bob went for two years and really enjoyed all of the Oxford principles. He loved all the people and he got everything down … except the not drinking part. He just stayed in terrible shape. They were all praying for him. They were all worried about him. You can see how important that preparation was for the arrival of another Oxford Grouper to arrive in Akron on a business deal—Bill Wilson.

There was a machine company based in Akron that made tools to make rubber, and it was in some trouble. Two groups were trying to get it. Bill was sent out there as an emissary from one group from Wall Street to see if they could take control of this company. Bill was promised that if they won, he would be the president of the company.

All the way out there he is planning. Pay off all the debts. Join the country club. I'll have the new car. I'll be playing golf again. He loved golf. My wife will be happy. She won't have to work in the department store. Amazing, alcoholics sometimes have these expectations. They've got their whole future over a proxy fight. Man, I'm on my way to being rich again. This is great. He's out there with about five and a half to six months' sobriety and he starts to think that this upswing will only take a little while … and then they lose the fight.

Now, he was broke. He was broke when he got there and he was still broke. He could hardly pay the hotel bill and he felt like maybe all this spirituality wasn't working that well. He started getting a little negative. He started thinking to himself, *This isn't fair. I'm trying as hard as I can to stay sober. I'm doing everything I can and look what happens to me. Nobody seems to care about my family and all the trouble I'm in. Maybe…*

And he listened to the bar people in the Mayflower Hotel and he could hear the music and the crowd was in there laughing. He said, *Maybe I ought to just go in there and have a few drinks of gin and be king for a day.*

He recognized how frightening that thought was because you know when that thought takes hold and starts getting going. So, he decided right there that the only way he was going to stay sober was to find another alcoholic to help. Many people say that this was one of the real origins of Alcoholics Anonymous. When an alcoholic realized that for him to stay sober himself, he had to go out and find another alcoholic to help.

He picked up the phone and he made these phone calls to people who have become part of our history. Reverend Tunks was the minister who had set up the whole Oxford Group thing in the first place, and he referred Bill to another man named Sheppard, who gave him some numbers of the Oxford Group people, including Henrietta Seiberling, daughter-in-law of the founder of the Goodyear Rubber Company.

She and Anne Smith were very close, and Bill called up and said, *I'm an Oxford Grouper from New York and I'm a recovered alcoholic. I need somebody to help.*

Henrietta Seiberling said, *My God, we've been praying for Dr. Bob to have something rescue him.* It is rumored that she said, "Yes, we've been expecting your call." There's possibly a little poetic license there, but in any event, she very excitedly called Anne Smith and said, *Get Dr. Bob over here. This is the moment. The man is here to save him.*

Anne said, *Well, I don't think he can be saved today. Saving will have to wait until tomorrow, because he went out to get me a Mother's Day plant. The plant is on the table, and Bob is under it.*

They had to wait until the next day. Dr. Bob slept most of the day, had a terrible hangover, and just was not feeling good. His wife nagged him to go see some guy from New York who wanted to talk to him about alcoholism. You can imagine—it was a Sunday, and he did not want to go talk to anybody.

On the way over to the gatehouse on the Seiberling estate, he promised her that he would talk for fifteen minutes. They sat down and talked for five and a half hours, one drunk talking to another. Dr. Bob was astounded. He didn't know anyone else felt like he did. He didn't know anybody else told the same lies. He didn't know anyone else drank like he did. He couldn't believe his eyes. This guy was like looking in the mirror—and the mirror was talking back.

There was that instant identification of one alcoholic talking to another. They talked and they talked and they talked. Henrietta Seiberling got Bill temporary quarters in one of the country clubs out there for about five days. Somebody paid off his bill in the Mayflower. When the week was up, he went to live with Dr. Bob, because he didn't have any money.

The two of them started trying to sober people up. Right away. They went down and tried to get one doctor, and that didn't work out. After about eight or nine days of this, Dr. Bob decided that, as he thought about his life, he was way behind on his medical education. There was an American Medical Association Convention in Atlantic City, and he thought maybe he ought to just get on that train and catch up on some of the courses that he missed. Of course, as soon as he got on the train, he got drunk.

He went to Atlantic City and he stayed drunk and came back. On June 10th, they dumped him out of the railroad car on the platform and called his wife to come get him. They carried him home. AA's birthday is in celebration of Dr. Bob lying on the railroad station floor having had AA's first slip, even though it wasn't AA yet.

Bill got him up. Dr. Bob had to perform a previously scheduled surgery. He gave him one beer to calm him down and some kind of a goofball pill to steady his hands, and he went in there and performed the surgery. Dr. Bob never had another drink.

Bill waited with Dr. Bob's wife, and they said, *When you're done, come on home and tell us how it went.* The surgery was in the morning, and pretty soon it was noon and he wasn't home. It was three in the afternoon, and he wasn't home. It was like five in the afternoon when he finally came in. They worried that he had gone back to drinking.

They asked him, *Where have you been?*

He said, *When I finished the surgery, I thought about my life. I realized that my drinking had hurt a lot of people here in Akron. I went around and made amends to them all.* That may be the record for how soon after your last drink you do your ninth step, because he did it all the same day.

In any event, that started the beginning of one alcoholic helping another, and we'll pick up on that next week and see how they started working there in Akron and simultaneously back in New York.

Now we get back to the principles. Having established in our first step that we are powerless, absolutely, over alcohol, we're confronted with something that generally drives all of us new people crazy. That is the concept of a Higher Power, of God. We came—I came—to believe that a power greater than ourselves could restore us to sanity.

After I first started, I liked the AA people, I liked my sponsor, I was having fun. We were going to meetings, and then we came to, *OK, now let's sit down, Sandy, and talk about God.*

I just said, *I don't think we want to do that. I am not comfortable* with that. *I just don't feel like I want to do that.* That's what our second step is all about: how to get to out of that box that we've been in with regard to this thing called "God" or "Spirit of the Universe" or "Higher Power" or whatever name we want to give it.

Many, even way back in the beginning, would say, *Well then just make the AA group your Higher Power. They certainly know more than you do about alcoholism, and you could certainly rely on them while you are trying to wrestle with this problem that you have in your mind about something bigger than yourself.*

As Bill wrote the literature, he addressed all the different types of us that arrived here. One type that arrives here goes to church all the time and prays, does novenas, and says rosaries—and is drunk all the time. They create the illusion that relying on God doesn't work. *I'm down there all the time, I am talking to the priest, and I'm drunk. No sense for me to try this God stuff. I'm already trying it, and it doesn't work.*

As it turns out, he wasn't really trying it. He was going through the motions. He was saying the words and showing up so that people would think that he was really trying, but in his heart, he had never really given spirituality a fair trial.

That's a funny thing for us who liked to claim that we're very logical. We like the scientific thing, not the spiritual stuff. We want to see it on a blackboard. Well, scientific experiments are designed to see what kind of results we get. Anybody with an open mind wouldn't mind performing experiments to see what might happen. Most of us have never given spirituality an experiment. We've never had an open mind: *OK, you really want me to try this?* We wrote it off without trying it because we were very smart. We knew that if we did try it, it wouldn't work, so why try it? Anybody think that way?

Some of us are so smart that we know what the experiment will produce without doing it. *The reason I don't pray is I already know if I pray, nothing will happen, so why should I pray if nothing is going to happen?* I thought that way all the time. I thought it was really smart. I found out that was not smart. It was stupid. There may be someone who doesn't know anything about God, churches—nothing. They have no experience whatsoever. Bill said, *Well, how are we going to approach that person?* One of the hardest tasks we have is to explain the situation to them, which he does in the beginning of step two in the Big Book.

If you are new, step two is not numbered in the Big Book. It is called the chapter to the agnostic, "We Agnostics." Of all places, the place to find God is in the chapter "We Agnostics."

When my sponsor gave me a Big Book and said, *Everything you need to know is in here,* I looked at it, and I just said, *Yeah, OK.* I mean, it was hard for me to believe that it was going to solve any of my problems. I did notice the chapter to the agnostics. I went through it and I made some marks and underlined a few things, so it would look like I read it.

When he came over and talked, I said, *Oh, yeah, I was reading it. It is really cool, right here, and I like this.* You didn't think I was going to take it seriously, did you? I knew what problems were and I knew what was necessary—money. That was the heart of all of my problems. When I saw the chapter to the agnostic, I said, being smart, *I know what that is. That's the chapter that tells the agnostics how to stay sober. It obviously doesn't include any steps.*

I knew I was going to eventually go to that chapter and find out how the agnostics stayed sober. Of course, when you read the chapter, it says, *Hey, if you're an agnostic, change your mind. Become a former agnostic.* Well, why should I do that? Why should I change my mind about spirituality and Higher Powers? Why should I change my mind?

He said, *Well, maybe you ought to read this.*

The first paragraph in that chapter says, "If when you drink you have little control over the amount you drink"—OK, that is everybody—"and if when you stop you can't stay stopped"—OK, that's everybody—"then you may be suffering from an illness that only a spiritual experience will help."

You are suffering from an illness that only a spiritual experience will help.

I told my sponsor, *Well, I don't believe in spiritual experiences.*

He said, *Well, then you're screwed. This is the situation that you are in.* It goes on to say, *To die an alcoholic death or to live on a spiritual basis are not easy alternatives to face.* That's the quote out of the Big Book.

If we had someone new here who was struggling with spirituality and alcoholism, we might make it into a quiz show and invite him up. *So, you want to be an alcoholic? Come on up, and we got two doors back here, Joe!* Joe is standing out in front. *You got to choose one of them. All right, All right. Now, let me show you door number one: die an alcoholic death. Do you want that door?*

No, I don't want that door, Sandy. Is there another door?

Yeah, live on a spiritual basis. Which door do you want?

If Joe is like the rest of us, he will stand there with his arms crossed thinking, *Alcoholic death or spiritual basis?*

Sounds like two pretty bad choices. Joe doesn't like either one.

Is there a third door?

No, there're only two doors.

Do I get a phone call?

Yes, you get a phone call.

So, Joe calls the family doctor and says, *Hey, Doctor, this is Joe. Listen, a friend of mine is curious. How bad is an alcoholic death?*

Oh God, it is really bad.

Joe hangs up. *OK, I'll do door number two.*

Why did you choose door number two?

Because door one is worse.

Joe is getting spiritual by default. He doesn't even believe in it. But there is nowhere else to go, so he accepts it.

And this is the beginning of spirituality. *OK, maybe I'll try it.* Now you know what that maybe is? It's the beginning of open-mindedness. *Maybe I'll try some of this.*

What can we look at that would help us in that situation? I'll tell you what I had to look at that was wonderful, and we don't have enough of it today. When I got sobered up in Washington D.C., we had seven speaker meetings for every discussion meeting. Every speaker meeting had two speakers. Ninety percent of the time, I was sitting in the audience listening to two stories. All the speakers said, *I was hopeless, and they told me how bad off I was, and now I'm doing great. It's because I changed my mind about a Higher Power.*

Then, the next speaker got up, and pretty soon some guy got up who was just like me, just like me. Spirituality just seemed unhelpful to me. I wouldn't touch that at the beginning. And then eventually I came in here and said, *OK, I'll try that stupid stuff. Hey it worked. I'm so happy. Everything is wonderful.*

What was in front of me was a steady collection of proof that I could not deny. That's the power of speaker meetings. You sit out there and you hear this story, and it's worse than yours. Sometimes I would hear these stories and I would think, *If this person doesn't get straightened out, that's a hopeless case.* Then, they would tell me, *So, I changed my mind. I tried this spiritual stuff and—my God. I got my health back and my family. I'm doing this, and now I'm doing that.*

This is what enables us to see spirituality. It's no longer a theory. We have visual proof right in front of us that this person, just like myself, somehow changed his mind about this God thing, and the rest is history. It is all right there in front of my eyes.

We come back and look at what it says. It says, "Came to believe that a power greater than ourselves could restore our sanity." That is what the process of coming to believe looks like. We just keep an open mind and then we watch. We see changes taking place. Then, maybe you start seeing them in yourself. You go, *I don't understand why I feel so terrible, I go to the noon meeting at YANA, and I feel better when I come out. Why is that? All they're doing is talking junk in there. Why should I feel better?* I don't know. Come up with an explanation. Could it be something called spiritual energy that heals people? Could it really be true that it's healing you?

When I first felt better, it made me nervous. I mean ... this stuff might work? Part of the thing I was afraid of was, *What if I prayed and it worked? Boy, would I look stupid. I have been bad mouthing prayer for twenty-five years. All my friends would give me a hard time. They would go, "See, you were wrong. You were wrong."*

Of course alcoholics hate being wrong. I would rather be right than anything. As long as I'm right, I won the argument. I would rather be right than happy.

Where do we get that rule? We have a whole program, as you are going to find out, where the real name of the game is "being wrong."

In the beginning, for an alcoholic to admit he's wrong is like turning the Queen Mary around in Tampa Harbor. It is a monumental thing for self-centered alcoholics to admit they're wrong.

The first time my sponsor said, *Look Sandy, you're wrong,* I said, *OK, you are right.*

No, you're wrong.

I said, *Well, it's the same thing.*

Well, say it.

It wouldn't come out. I was wrong about spirituality, and so is everybody who never gave it a fair chance. That's all that is required.

Can you suddenly come from a stubborn no to a maybe? Could I possibly begin to actually allow myself to think that there could be a power greater than myself that would make its presence known to me personally? Not through somebody else. Not through some minister telling me that this power exits, but to actually experience it. There's a big difference between knowing about a spiritual power and experiencing it.

There was this story about a sociologist who found a lost tribe in a cave system. They didn't know anything about modern civilization. The sociologist decided to take ten or twenty years to bring these people into the modern world instead of bringing a TV in that day, because the shock would be too great. They were in this cave system and they had fires and they were able to fish, but they'd never been outside. They knew about fire and eating.

So, they started explaining the outside world, and they started learning how to speak to them in their language and teaching the people English. This process went on, and they decided that one of the most important things that they would have to teach them about was electricity, because when they came out they were going to see elevators going up and down, lights going on, *everything*. So, they were deciding what the best way was to teach people about electricity. There were two schools of thought, and the two schools remind me of the AA way of teaching about spirituality and the church way.

The number one way was to slowly educate them out of textbooks about electricity—start with ohms and watts and resistance. It's going to take years, but eventually we could get a few people up to maybe the sophomore in college level of electricity and then have them take a test. Then they'd know, yes, they understand electricity.

Now, method number two was a little simpler than that. They decided to put a generator outside, run a wire in, and bring an electric lamp in. They'd connect the lamp, hand them a bulb, and say, *Turn the bulb in the socket*. And then what would happen? All of a sudden, *boom*! There'd be light. And the scientists would say, *You see that? That's electricity. Now we want to show you one more thing.* So they would unscrew the bulb and say, *Now stick your finger in the socket.*

That is personal experience with electricity as opposed to a theory about its alleged existence. AA fits in the second category in the experiment with spirituality. We use the steps in order to get you to stick your finger in the light socket, and then you personally experience something. You can call it anything that you want. That's what the second step is designed to do. To enable us to have a personal relationship, a personal awareness, that returns us to sanity.

Sanity is described as soundness of mind. I'll tell you what I think it means. I think that until a human being experiences the actual awareness of their own creator, they are all insane, because they are seeing the world in a way that isn't true. That is simply manufactured, made up by the ego, and we live in this frightening place where there is no Higher Power. We're not even *aware* of it. It's just a rumor.

When the connection is made, the power comes in to enable us to see how wonderful people are. To see how wonderful AA is. We suddenly look around and we go, *Well, all these other people, they're just like me. I'm part of AA. I'm not apart from AA. I'm a part of it.* That awareness, that little awakening, is the beginning of no longer existing apart from the universe, our friends, and our Higher Power.

We find out that the only problem we have, according to Chuck C—and I'll talk about this a lot later on—is conscious separation from God, our fellow human beings, and the universe. We actually believe that we exist apart from all this, and it's very frightening. As this energy comes in, we realize that we don't exist apart from, but we are a part of. Isn't it funny that *apart* as one word means "separated from" and when it's two words it means "part of"?

Rather than being apart, we are a part of.

When you become a part of something, it's a beautiful place to live.

3

Just Judge the Results

WE LEFT OFF in telling the story of Alcoholics Anonymous getting started with how two people from Vermont started this great social program in Akron, Ohio, which is just the most wonderful irony in the world. After staying there for a while, they called on AA number three, Bill Dotson, who was a lawyer. Then they got a guy named Ernie Galbraith sober. Dr. Bob kept working, looking for drunks in Akron, and Bill went back to New York and worked on drunks in that area. When he got back, Bill was by himself, and he had this idea of trying to get something going to help alcoholics all over the place. He had about seven months' sobriety himself and he was broke. He didn't even have a job and he was trying to figure out how in the world to make this work.

A funny thing happened because of two guys who came out of Towns Hospital. One of them had been there nine times before; this was his tenth time. The other one was there for his first time. When they were released, they both joined the Oxford Group. They had a little bit of sobriety, and when they met Bill, they both immediately took to his ideas. They just said, *Oh, my God, we want to be part of that team.*

I think it was very important that Bill ran into these two; Fitz Mayo and Hank Parkhurst. Both of their stories are in the first edition of the Big Book. Hank is the unbeliever, and Fitz Mayo is the southern gentleman. Fitz's father was a minister in Virginia, and he was more of the intellectual type—he liked to think about things. He made a nice addition when Bill needed perspective on things. Meanwhile, Hank Parkhurst was a bull, a hard-charging salesman. He managed people. He was in charge. He had been a football player. He was just, *Let's go!* You just didn't sit down and discuss the strategy, you went full speed ahead, which was a nice combination to have at this stage of the game.

We talk now about, *Well, somebody only has two years. Do we want them to lead the meeting?* Or, *Well, he only has two years, and maybe he shouldn't speak yet at an open meeting.* But with a little under two years' sobriety, Fitz went and started AA in Washington, D.C., and it became incredibly successful. They had all kinds of meetings there by 1940, and he remained a constant supporter of AA activity. He would go to Akron and come to New York whenever he was needed to review the Big Book, to do whatever was necessary.

But Bill's real partner was Hank Parkhurst. This was the guy that got things going. Shortly after he got sober, in the Oxford Group, members really had their spiritual awakening. They went in those rooms and were asked, *Do you believe in God?* I mean, they got on their knees, and God Bless America, it was cranked up. He got up and testified. He was really fired up about sobriety.

He had a convertible car that he drove Bill and Fitz around in. They were driving down Park Avenue one night, and Bill looked over and Hank was standing up while he was driving and shouted out, *God Almighty, booze was never as good as this!* He really was into his spiritual awakening and how wonderful it made him feel. He was just as fired up as Bill was about sharing this.

We got to get this word out to the alcoholics that are still suffering!

He tied right in with Bill's idea that what we needed most of all was money. That was the secret to everything. I mean, how are you going to get a worldwide organization together without money? Bill worked on Wall Street, so you can see his plan was for a chain of drunk tanks, because the hospitals were getting upset when you tried to get alcoholics sober there. They threw up all over the other patients, and it was hard for hospitals to have a policy of accepting people to dry out. So he wanted a chain of drunk tanks. Then he wanted the drunks to quit their jobs and travel around the country starting AA in different cities. That was going to take dough. So they figured they'd have to pay for these guys like paid missionaries. Eventually, they'd need a book so that everyone would be singing from the same page. But the book wasn't the big thing in the beginning. The big thing was raising money, and Hank was his buddy.

They spent about a whole year trying to raise money, and they got nothing. They got nothing. They'd go to foundations. They'd go to rich people in New York and Bill's connections from Wall Street, and people would say, *Well, what are you talking about, a couple of drunks? I mean, I'd rather give to the Boy Scouts or something like that. I just don't see it.* They didn't raise anything.

Bill had a brother-in-law who was a doctor, and was a very important player in Bill's sobriety because he kept paying for him to go to Towns Hospital. He probably wouldn't have made it without his brother-in-law's money. He and Hank were commiserating with him. Bill's brother-in-law had met somebody from the Rockefeller Office the previous year, and Bill thought his brother-in-law could call this guy.

So he called him up, and it turned out to be Rockefeller's personal secretary, the guy who made all the decisions on what went in front of John Rockefeller to look at, at the Rockefeller Foundation. His name was Willard Richardson and he said, *Come on over.* They didn't even have to wait. Bill got on the elevator in Rockefeller Center or wherever headquarters was, and he got out on Rockefeller's floor.

He was thinking, *The dough is near. We are close to the jackpot.* The two of them started telling Richardson about this thing— using spiritual principles to help drunks get sober.

We got about fifteen of us that are in Akron and here and…

Richardson, who looked at a lot of worthy causes, thought this one was a real winner and that Rockefeller would love it.

He said, *Could you guys come back and meet with the trustees and the big advisers?*

Oh, yeah.

So, they had a big meeting in the conference room, and they described all this. The trustees and advisers said, *Let's send a couple of guys out to Akron so they can do a written report for Mr. Rockefeller.* They went out and they talked to Dr. Bob, they went to the hospital and they saw the work that was being done, and they typed up this report and gave it to Mr. Rockefeller.

Willard Richardson was called in, and Rockefeller said, *This looks like a very wonderful thing. I don't know when I've ever been moved by something like this. But I think money will spoil it. Now, I'll be willing to donate a few dollars so these guys don't get their homes foreclosed, and this Mr. Wilson and Dr. Smith can have $30 a month so that they can hang in there. But I honestly think large amounts of money would be a big mistake.*

This didn't sit well with Hank and Bill.

But as it turns out, it was God's plan that we didn't get money in here. They formed an Alcoholic Foundation, because Bill decided, in spite of what Rockefeller said, they had to raise money. The way to raise it was to have a foundation, and they got some of the people from the Rockefeller Foundation to be on the board.

So now they went out with the Alcoholic Foundation and they were going here and going there ... and they're going nowhere. Now, in order to raise money, Bill had written two chapters that ended up in our Big Book: "A Vision for You" and "Bill's Story." He used these two chapters when he was hitting up people for dough. He would leave that with them. He had a multilith copy [*a small printing press —Ed.*], and he would go in there and go, *Well, we've got this organization—here, read this. Read about what's going to be happening.* And even after they read them, nobody gave any money.

But somebody that Bill knew said, *Why don't you take those two chapters down to Harper's Publishing and talk to the religious editor down there? See what he thinks.*

They took it down there, and the religious editor said, *This is very good. We'd like to publish a book like this. Do you think you can finish this book?*

Bill said, *Of course, I'll have it done very soon.*

They offered him $1,500 as an advance. Boy, did that sound good.

This was back in 1938, and that was a lot of money. And when you're broke, it's really a lot of money. But Hank Parkhurst talked Bill out of it. *We don't want them having the profits off of this book. We want to keep this for ourselves. We can form our own publishing company and then we'll make all the money.*

Bill kind of went, *Yeah, that is a good idea, and we'll make the money.*

Of course, it's so hard to publish a book or to get anything like this started, but those two power-drivers were ready to go. Hank went in and got some stock certificates and a blank letter of incorporation. They didn't get it incorporated for a couple years. But he wrote out stock certificates in the Works Publishing Company for a value of $25. You could make payments over five months of $5 a month, and they went to the AA meetings selling the stock certificates to the drunks. (Well, they weren't AA meetings, they were the Oxford meetings, plus the alcohol squad that met at Bill's house. They also met in the restaurant after meetings. So, there was the meeting after the meeting even when it was the Oxford.)

The drunks said, *You want us to buy stock in a book that ain't written yet? I don't think so.* They knew they had to get something, so Hank and Bill went to Pleasantville where the Reader's Digest was headquartered. They talked to one of the editors there and told them about this book and this organization.

The editor said, *My God, that's exactly what Reader's Digest loves! We love doing human interest stories, and yes, I think we'd be very interested in this!*

Hank said, *And you'll mention the book?*

He said, *Yes, yes, we'll mention the book. You call me when the book is finished, and we'll get ready to go.*

Well, now, they went back to the Oxford drunks and they said, *Boys, we've done some checking here. We checked with the printer— they can print one of these books for 35 cents, and we're going to sell them for $3.50, a thousand percent profit. We've gone up to Reader's Digest, and they're going to run a story about this book as soon as it's finished, and they have 12 million readers. So here's your chance, boys—these books are going to go out in carload lots. You are going to get rich!*

Well, they sold a few here and a few there, and Charlie Towns from Towns Hospital dropped in a couple thousand dollars. Slowly the book project was moving along. It got quite a bit along and so they had to hand out the chapters to write. All the writing was now going on; authorship of the chapters is debated, and you can look at different history books as to who wrote what. But clearly, Bill wrote a great deal of it. Hank Parkhurst wrote the chapter "To the Employer"; at the beginning of that, he talks about being an executive in a large corporation with 6,600 employees—that was his job with Standard Oil. Also, Bill and Hank edited the twelve stories from the New York people, much to their resentment. (Because they didn't check with them about changing the stories, they just changed them to make them sound better in the book.)

Out in Akron they had a newspaperman who edited the stories out there. So they got a pretty good draft and they put it together. They had a heck of a falling out over "How It Works." Bill hated to write that chapter. He said, *Oh, my God, I don't want to do that, because there was enough controversy over everything else.*

But he finally was sitting there looking at the six tenets of the Oxford Group, which is basically what they were using, and he started thinking that the drunks were sneaking through the loopholes in those six tenets. So he started with a legal pad and a pencil to close the loopholes so the drunks couldn't wiggle out. When he got through, he felt very spiritually wonderful because it ended up twelve. There were twelve apostles. There were twelve months in a year. *Because this looks very spiritual, I'm glad it ended up twelve.* So you can see it was just totally arbitrary, but he made a big deal out of it.

When he circulated it, all hell started breaking loose. Hank and Jim Burwell of New York did not want a religious-type program (Jim was a reformed Atheist). They wanted a psychological program—so you'd talk about the psychological problems of the alcoholic and then you could slowly work in some spiritual stuff. But, in their opinion, it would scare all the drunks off, so we couldn't have that. That's the New York crowd. Now out in Akron, they wanted to just have it be Jesus. Why beat around the bush? So you've got these two factors going: *It's going to be Jesus. No, it's going to be nothing.*

Out of that terrible conflict came *God as I understand it.* That solved the problem because it satisfied the New York guys. They really got this thing going. They had the multilith; they sent it around to a few people to look at. They sent it to the Catholic Committee on Publications, who thought it was pretty good. They wanted one thing changed in Bill's story—where he said that he was catapulted into heaven. They felt that the Catholic Church was the direction to get to heaven and that they had promised that to all of their people. Would he mind changing that word? So he did. He changed it to utopia. If you're ever reading that, you'll know that the Catholics got their little finger in the pie after all.

They're all set now, so they go back to Reader's Digest and they go, *Mr. Blackwell, we're ready to shoot.*

He said, *Shoot what?*

Bill said, *The book! We got the book ready.*

Oh, you're the guys that came up here about six months ago. Yeah, oh, yeah—I remember you guys now. You know, I thought it was a great idea, but when I talked to the senior editors, they didn't like the idea at all, and I forgot to call you.

Now, they had all these loans and the stock certificates out and they couldn't pay the printer. So, one of them, an Irishman named Ryan, had a friend who knew Gabriel Heatter. Gabriel Heatter had a radio show that was kind of like 1930s Larry King. Everybody listened. During the show he always had a human interest thing. They called him up and, by God, Heatter would get Ryan on there, and Ryan would talk about his recovery and the book. This was all set, but Ryan had a tendency to slip, and the radio show wasn't for ten days. Bill got four big guys and put Ryan in the New York Athletic Club under guard night and day. Ryan made it to *The Gabriel Heatter Show*, and it did help some of the orders to come in. But it was a very difficult thing and very close. I won't go into all the details, but it did finally make it, with some loans from one guy from Baltimore and another one from Dr. Silkworth.

Then something bad happened. Hank had been Bill's partner from the day they met. Hank had an office. He was still in the oil business even though he had been fired from Standard Oil. He had an office over in New Jersey, and he and Bill came up with this idea of forming a co-op, so that the Northern New Jersey gasoline dealers could buy at great quantity and save money. It was called The Honor Dealers. Hank had hired a secretary, Ruth Hock.

Bill would come over to work on this business. It wasn't long before all Ruth saw were drunks coming in there to get sobered up—there wasn't any oil business going on. Then when they got the idea for the book, guess who typed our Big Book? Ruth Hock. Bill would dictate, and she would type, then he'd come back with corrections, and she would retype it and retype it. They were broke, so they didn't have much money to pay her salary, but they would give her stock certificates in the Works Publishing Company, not yet incorporated.

Here's another stock certificate, Ruth. Go ahead and keep typing. This is going to be worth a lot of money someday. Everything was just hanging in the balance. Hank was going through troubles with his wife, and it got worse and worse. In the middle of that, he took a liking to Ruth, and the two of them started dating a little bit.

Hank's wife sued him for everything that he had and called him a lot of bad names. He came into the office feeling terrible and told Ruth he really wanted to marry her. Ruth said, *No, I can't do that. I want to keep working on this book project.*

That really irked Hank that his buddy Bill was taking his girlfriend away from him to work on the project. He did what any good alcoholic would do in situation like that—he got drunk. It caused a lot of serious problems for Alcoholics Anonymous. He got drunk. He would come in the office and threaten people. The rest of the office eventually wanted to move into New York where Bill was, and without checking with Hank, they did move all the furniture to New York. Bill had decided that there was enough money to buy back all the shares in the Works Publishing Company, which would give the Big Book to Alcoholics Anonymous and there wouldn't be any shareholders, except for Hank's shares. Hank came in drunk and upset, saw the furniture gone, and accused Bill of stealing it.

Bill said, *Well, listen, why don't I give you $200 for that furniture and you hand over the stocks?* Hank was desperate, so he handed them over. Then he went out to Cleveland to get a little sympathy from his brother-in-law, Clarence Snyder.

Now, Clarence was Mr. AA in Cleveland. I'm going to tell you some stories about Clarence later. But he was really amazing. He didn't like the idea of a centralized AA. He didn't like Bill Wilson getting all the publicity. *Oh, Bill Wilson, Bill Wilson, Bill Wilson—you know, it's like Jesus!* Clarence had started the first Intergroup, he had done the first pamphlets, he had written stuff on everything and he was really an amazing Twelve-Stepper, one of the great contributors to our program. But he also was sympathetic to Hank, and he listened to Hank's version of how he got cheated out of the money that was coming from the Big Book.

And then Hank said, *Now Dr. Bob and Bill are going to get rich. Besides that, I know they're doing something with the Rockefellers. I think Rockefeller secretly gave them $64,000.*

Do you ever wonder why Dr. Bob wrote "Gossip"? You have

to watch that in his last talk; he said, "Let us also remember to guard that erring member - the tongue, and if we must use it, let's use it with kindness and consideration and tolerance." [*From Dr. Bob's brief remarks on Sunday, July 30, 1950, at the First International A.A. Convention, in Cleveland, Ohio. –Ed.*] Gossip did a lot of damage right here. As a matter of fact, Dr. Silkworth took a look at Hank Parkhurst and told Bill that he thought he was getting paranoid and that he might be dangerous.

He caused much trouble out there. Hank took his cause and went to all the Cleveland groups and said, *My friend tells me what's going on in New York, and they're making a lot of money—they got a deal with Rockefeller.* They just repeated a lot of things that really weren't true. Then the word started coming into New York that the Cleveland groups were going to leave the big organization and go out on their own.

Dr. Bob and Bill went out to Cleveland to talk to the people, and they held a regular dinner with the speakers. They spoke, and there appeared to be some sort of understanding. But as soon as that part was over, four or five of the Cleveland guys said, *Now we want to meet you two over here in this other room.* And in that other room were a lawyer and a CPA, and they were armed to the teeth with evidence of these terrible wrongdoings that were going on. In other words, they were really ambushed—they had no idea this was coming.

But Bill had brought with him all the financial records. At the end of the thing they just said, *All right, well, here, we'll turn them over.* These records told the truth about their current financial status. Bill and Bob were both broke. They were getting $35 to $50 a month, and there was nothing else coming in. The whole thing was not true. The people that were there apologized and accepted that, but the buzz continued for years that *those guys in New York, they were up to something and we know.* It took quite a while for that to settle down. You can see when you started something in AA— especially back when AA was so new—it was frightening because the whole thing could collapse, and so many people were already relying on AA to stay sober.

Hank never really got sober again. He had a few years here and there, but they could never resume their friendship. He died in 1954. But having said all of that, he was one of the main players in ensuring that our organization got started. His enthusiasm and the way he just didn't take no for an answer got us over a lot of hurdles that we should be grateful for. Fitz, the southern gentleman, actually brought AA to Maryland and Washington, D.C. and was one of the great characters that we had in the early history. The last one that I mentioned earlier was Ernie Galbraith. Ernie has his own claim to fame. He eloped with Dr. Bob's daughter, when he had about three months' sobriety, which did not go over well with Dr. Bob.

So this outrageous behavior on the part of newcomers started early, didn't it? Don't get in a relationship for the first twelve months—OK, Dr. Bob.

Anyway, that's where we'll leave it off in our little drama about the unfolding of the AA story to get back on the spiritual path with these principles.

Sometimes it's helpful to jump all the way to the last step. It's like reading the ending of a book and going back to read the rest of it. The last step tells us what the point of the other steps is. If you know that ahead of time, then you can see what this is all about.

The last step says, "Having had a spiritual awakening as the result of these steps..." One result is all that's talked about. You get a spiritual awakening as the result of these steps. "...We tried to carry the message to alcoholics." What message? How to have a spiritual awakening. It's very important to note, that's the message that we're passing on. Not just how to stay sober, but how to transform yourself so that sobriety is fun and that the world looks different. That's the point of the whole thing.

As we go back to the beginning, we can see that we're taking a series of actions that will cause this to happen. Recall Dr. Jung's quote about religion: "The primary job of religion is to keep the people away from direct contact with God." AA is just the opposite. The point here is to have your own personal experience. We talk about surrendering—and it has to be 100 percent, or nothing else will happen. Then we talked about the debate process of slowly allowing ourselves to say *maybe* to believing that there's a Higher Power—to really get honest and tell ourselves we never did give spirituality a fair shake. We laughed at it. We gave it lip service, but we never really did give this thing a fair trial. We're in a situation where unless this works, we're probably going to die, so why not give it a shot?

That's where we are able to come to believe in a power greater than ourselves restoring us to sanity. We make a decision to turn our will and our lives over to the care of this power. *God as we understand Him*—this came out of that big argument between Akron and New York.

That sounds almost impossible. *I see. I'm going to turn my life over to something that I don't even know exists. I am going to turn over my life.* I mean, geez that just sounds too mysterious. It sounds too far out.

I made a decision to turn my life over. Well, let's take a look at our lives prior to doing that. We're running our own lives. We're not turning them over to anything. We are the final arbiters of every single thing that we do. Nobody tells me what to do, I decide. I am the one who makes all the decisions about my life.

If you have the type of sponsor I have, he says, *Hey, how's it going?*

If you're honest, you say, *Not good.* Now, there's a beginning.

My sponsor said, *If we could get you to stop doing it, we would remove the management of your life from an idiot.*

So, if we can't believe in anything else, we could believe that if I stop running it, it's probably going to improve. Self-centeredness. Bill goes into that in the Big Book. Self-centeredness is the root of our problems. Self-centeredness. Selfishness. We step on people's feet.

We're in constant conflict with everybody around us. Selfishness. Self-centeredness.

They say it enough and finally you go, *OK, I'll go along with that. All right, I am self-centered. I've known it for a long time but I've never admitted it.*

All self-centered people make the following statement once they admit they're self-centered: *I'm going to do something about that. I'm going to damn well do something about being self-centered.*

Oh, good, what are you actually going to do?

Well, I'm going to focus on not being self-centered.

I say, *You are going to sit there focused on not being the center?*

Yes.

Well, when you look at it, you think, *That's impossible. I'm still the center of becoming un-self-centered. It's just a joke to think that I can become un-self-centered.* The only answer possible is to find something else to be the center. In the beginning, it's liable to be our sponsor. *I'll make my sponsor be the center of my life and I'll let him or her make all the decisions for me on my behalf.* Gently under our breath, we say, *Until I get my act together, and then I'll take it back.* But we don't say that out loud. We're making a little concession in this direction, you can see that?

Then we go, *Well, yeah, with respect to alcohol, it makes sense, this AA Program. They know a lot more about alcohol. So, I'm going to take this little alcohol chunk and turn that over. So there's a big step in the right direction. But with all other areas of my life, I think I'll still keep them.* I always love this sentence: *If I turn everything over, I will be the hole in the doughnut. I will be a non-entity. I will have nothing to do, because right now my full-time job is running my life. So, this whole thing is, my God, I'm going to turn this over?*

Well, a lot of times we come in here and we talk about being a slave to alcohol—that alcohol got a hold of us and all of a sudden it totally controlled our lives. We really didn't have a say in how things were going. I wanted to not have a drink, but there was nothing I could do about it. As soon as I drank, I didn't know what was going to happen. It was up to the alcohol. I might wake up in my own hometown or two states over. I was being directed by alcohol, and I desperately wanted my freedom back. We hear a lot about freedom and choice. *I want my choice back and my freedom.* So when we get to AA and we get free from alcohol, now we got what we asked for: freedom.

Now I can do anything I want. Let's see, what should I do? What would be best for me? Well, maybe, this plan. So I tried that, and people were in my way. They were blocking me. I can't get there—maybe this would be a better plan. It turns out that freedom is not all it's cracked up to be.

It's a big struggle.

I'm free to do anything, all my choices are here. I'm standing right here, I can go 360 different directions. But I can't figure out which one is best for me. So right now I'm standing still.

This is what we get back, and when we first get it, we go, *I love it. I'm not trapped in there. I'm not a slave to alcohol anymore.*

Bill goes on. I wonder how independent we really are? Are we independent of our character defects? Are we making the decision, or is greed making the decision? Are we making the decision, or is pride making the decision? Am I making this decision freely, or is lust influencing me? Am I not, in fact, being jerked around by all my character defects, even when I'm sober? Am I in a constant state of frustration and anger, restless, irritable, discontent, sober? I'm being yanked around by all these forces—my life is a mess with all of this freedom! What am I going to do about that?

Now, the funny thing is the highest pay grade in Alcoholics Anonymous is *servant*. A servant is someone who willingly allows a power greater than ourselves to tell us what to do. A slave doesn't have any choice. They are forced to do the work whether they want to or not. Ironically, the jobs that a slave and a servant do sometimes look very similar. Both of them are sweeping the floor. Both of them are picking up boxes in a supermarket (which a lot of us drunks do when we're new). Only the servant is happily doing it because it was their choice. It was their choice to give up their choice.

So as Bill explores this in both the Big Book and the Twelve and Twelve, he discusses how independent we really are. Maybe we just think we're independent, and here we encounter the second spiritual paradox of our program. The first being that we win by giving up. That victory is achieved through surrender. Now we're going to find out that true independence is achieved by becoming dependent on a loving Higher Power. That the best possible life for me would be one that was guided by my own Creator, my own loving Creator, who knows way beyond I do what's best for me.

This step is the beginning of this process, and nothing gets turned over in the third step. I remember reading it and then going, *I have to get my life turned over, over, turn over, OK, over, over.* When you're new, you do really weird things, so I always tried to do these things in front of a mirror—I figured the facial expression was crucial in whether your life was turned over or not. So I'd get in front of a mirror: *God, you got it. God, you got it.* So no matter what I did, I didn't feel like anything happened. I mean, I was turning and turning and turning—*God, you got it. God, take it. God, you got it, got it, got it, gone, gone, gone*—and there I am, still in charge.

It didn't say that we got anything turned over. It says we made a decision to turn our life over, which is like making a decision to get a college degree. There's still some work to do before we get the degree. What that leaves us with is the rest of the steps between us and our own Creator. As we leave this step and begin this journey, the whole journey will depend on how earnestly we are trying to turn our life over.

Bill makes an interesting comment in the Twelve and Twelve where he talks about willpower. It's the first time I think it shows up in the literature. And, of course, if you have a sponsor like I do, you know there's no way you can stay sober on willpower. Don't even think about it. I mean, drunks just can't resist alcohol, so don't even think that this can be done by willpower. Then it turns out that the only way to do it is by willpower. That sounds like you're talking out of both sides of your mouth. Well, you can't directly achieve sobriety through your own willpower, but it takes willpower to go to meetings. It takes willpower to buy the Big Book and read it. It takes willpower to do the steps. I have to make this choice. So, Bill puts in the Twelve and Twelve that this is the proper use of the will, to bring it in harmony with that of our Higher Power.

He also talks about free will, which I've always been interested in. I've often wondered if I ever had free will, because it seemed like my character defects were always jerking me around. Then there's the influence of my parents, the influence of the church, the influence of what I had read—how do I know whether I am free to make any kind of a choice? That debate could go on forever about determinism and free will.

I'll make you a bet on this one: There is one area where we have free will, absolute, complete free will. We can either choose God or not choose God. That is absolutely up to us. What is suggested here is you have gotten this far by not choosing God. That was all of us. We may have heard about it before. But we never chose it, we just abandoned it. I stopped going to church on Sunday because I was too drunk on Saturday night. What is left here is, *Why don't you try choosing God, the Higher Power, and then see what kind of results you get?*

My point to anybody new is, your job is no longer to manage your life. You follow the guidance from your sponsor and your group and from the literature in our spiritual program. You have a huge job, though. Your job is to keep very careful track of the results and report back on whether things are getting worse or better. Just jot them down.

Wow, another month went by, and I seem to be better. First, we don't want to admit it because then we'd be wrong. Because we already told everybody this wasn't going to work. *That kind of stuff doesn't work for me, it doesn't work for me.* When it did work, I remember I didn't want to tell my sponsor I was secretly getting happy from praying. Because I knew all my buddies would jump out and go, *Hahahaha!* But I was. There is nothing like personal results to convince us of the reality of this program and our own Creator.

If you're at this step, turn everything over, except judging the results. I think you're going to find that you're off for a heck of a good ride. I tell new people that I sponsor that there's only one question you should ever ask: *What should I do next?* That's it. *I'm up here now, what should I do next?*

Now, if you do that, whatever it is, you have to become willing. *Oh, you want me to go early and make their coffee? You don't want to do that?* The second you say, *OK,* you feel like a million dollars. You feel like a million dollars. No more resistance. No more barriers to all this stuff.

I'm a player. Count me in. Never thought I'd join a dirt bag organization like this, but OK. All right, I'm a member. That is when happiness begins. *I'll do it,* instead of, *No, never.*

Oh, it's so lonely out in *no, never* land. Oh, it's terrible out there. Many of us spent a lot of time out there. Finally, we had to swallow our pride, come back.

What do you want me to do?

And that was the beginning of quite a nice life. So, whenever you can, just go, *OK.*

4

It's the Projector, Stupid

EARLY ON, THERE were a couple of publications that informed people about Alcoholics Anonymous (because AA doesn't promote itself and hire an advertising agency), and one of them was Liberty Magazine, where there was a story, "Alcoholics and God." It was a religious thing, and it did get a few inquiries, but not as many as the other one. The other one concerned a baseball player for the Cleveland Indians named Rollie Hemsley. Rollie Hemsley was an all-star catcher in the '30s and '40s for the Cleveland Indians. He caught for Bob Feller; when I was growing up, if someone said, "Bob Feller," you went, "That's the fastest pitch there is." He was a pretty famous pitcher.

Well, Hemsley's performance as a baseball player began to drop off significantly as his alcoholism progressed. He was able to keep it under control for a while, but as time took its toll, his performance slacked and his batting average dropped. The manager of the Cleveland Indians became concerned and he, through a friend or some little story, heard about the Oxford Group.

So, he went to the Oxford Group and he said, *How much to get Hemsley sober? Because he's a very valuable player to us, and we will pay good dollars to get him sober.*

Of course, the Oxford Group is going, *No, there's no money involved, but he has to join an Oxford Group. We are getting some* alcoholics sober in these groups. *As a matter of fact, we have a hospital in Akron, which is where he has to start out.* Of course that was with Dr. Bob down at St. Thomas Hospital in Akron.

The manager said, *Well, he won't go to a hospital. There's no way. I've tried to talk to him, but you see, he doesn't like that. He's not going to go to a hospital.*

The Oxford Group says, *Well, unless he goes there, there's nothing that can be done.*

So, they finagled with an opposing pitcher to deliberately hit him, and then the trainer ran out—it was a very minor injury, but he declared that he had to go to the hospital. So off they shipped him down to Akron, and he had no idea what was coming, but he was on his way to getting sober. Which he did.

As he developed one and two years' sobriety moving into 1941, his performance on the field skyrocketed. His batting average goes up and he's not making any errors and he's throwing people out at second and it was … *wow.*

So, the reporters were coming around and they're going, *To what do you owe this? How come you're suddenly doing so well?*

He said, *Oh, I joined Alcoholics Anonymous, and everything is turning out wonderful.*

And they said, *Oh really? Well, tell us all about it.*

Well it's a little organization. I go down and they … it's just amazing what they're doing.

That story went in all kinds of major newspapers in the sports sections, and sporting enthusiasts (alcoholics) read it. Some of them said, *Well, if it's good enough for Rollie Hemsley, it's good enough for me.* So, we see an early example of anonymity breaks doing some good. They didn't really capture the anonymity principle until a little bit later. In the beginning, people were getting their picture taken, and when they did the Jack Alexander article in the *Saturday Evening Post*, there was a picture taken of AA members.

Now, the other character that played a predominant role at this time was a very famous AA member who got sober in

1938—probably AA number ten or eleven—and his name was Clarence Snyder. Clarence's story is absolutely amazing. I think he was born in 1902, and Clarence was a super everything. Super salesman, super anything—from athlete to dancer, you just name it. Until drinking came along and he was one of those alcoholics that—*Wham!*—when it hit, it hit like a ton of bricks.

He had gotten married, and his wife (who also joined AA later on) became very concerned with his drinking. He'd been fired from everything, and she was trying to get him to go to a hospital. He was just drinking around the clock like a crazy man and totally unpredictable; she was thinking of having him locked up, really reaching her last straw with him. Her brother was a truck driver. She said to her brother, *What if you have Clarence stay with you in the truck? If you keep him up in that compartment on the top of the truck while you drive all over the country, there's no way that he can get drunk.* Which is true.

So, they started off on this trucking route. The thing there, of course, is that after a few days without a drink, he was going nuts in there. He was trying to dream up things to tell his brother-in-law. His brother-in-law was tired, and Clarence said, *Look, why don't you go get a meal, freshen up, and I'll guard the truck while you're gone?* Of course, guarding the truck included going down to some gin mill and getting some cheap whiskey; his brother-in-law finds him drunk guarding his truck. That ended the relationship. They were on their way to New York City, and the brother-in-law just dumped Clarence on the streets in New York City.

Clarence tried to survive in New York, and he had a sister-in-law that lived there whom he had befriended earlier and had done a lot of things for. I mean, he really saved her house and did some tremendous things, and he figured she owed him a favor.

So, he called her and said, *Do you remember all the things I did? Maybe I could come by.*

Oh yeah, sure, Clarence. She wasn't aware of the exact condition that he was in. When he came over, she just slammed the door on him and just said, *I'm sorry but I'm not helping you. You just stay out there.*

Somehow, he worked his way back to Ohio and decided to return to his wife, and he came home. She looked at him through the door and knew better than to open it. She just started telling him, *No, you're not coming in. I know it sounds hard, but you're not getting in.*

He said, *I hope I'm going to die. It's hopeless. It's hopeless.* The funny thing is that her sister had called her telling her that Clarence had been there and also that she had heard from a doctor in New York that there was another doctor in Akron that could help Clarence. The doctor in New York was Bill's brother-in-law, Leonard Strong, who was a big player in getting Bill to see Rockefeller. He paid for Bill to go to Towns Hospital. His name is pretty well known in AA history. That's where Clarence found out about Dr. Bob—through Bill's brother-in-law.

Anyway, he hemmed and hawed about going down there, trying to get his wife to give him the travel money to go to Akron on the bus. She knew if she gave him the travel money to go to Akron, he would drink the travel money and he would still be there outside her door in Cleveland.

So, she went down to the bus company with him, bought the ticket and made him get on while she was watching, to be sure that they stamped the ticket and he couldn't get a refund out of it. Then she followed the bus to the first stop … through the two other stops in Cleveland until it hit the main road for Akron. Off he went and was dumped out there and finally made his way to see Dr. Bob.

They checked him into the hospital. This is how the Oxford Group worked back then. They checked him into the hospital, and he recovered physically for three or four days. Then, Dr. Bob came by—he was a big man—and he said, *All right, son, you're ready.*

He said, *Ready for what?*

He said, *Ready for God. Son, I want to know something. I want to know it right now. Do you believe in God?*

Well, I don't know. I'm not sure.

No, you can't be not sure. You either believe or you don't. Now what's your decision?

Well, maybe. I guess…

No, you don't guess so. Yes or no?

That's a lot of pressure when you're sitting in a little short nighty on a bed with four days' sobriety. He said, *OK, I do.*

OK, get on your knees.

Why?

Because we're going to pray.

In this little short nighty?

Yeah. Get down on the floor.

They got down on their knees, and Dr. Bob looked up and said, *Jesus, this is Clarence Snyder. He's a drunk. Clarence, this is Jesus. You ask Him to help you stop drinking and to manage your life.*

OK. Jesus, could you please manage my life and help me keep sober?

Then, Dr. Bob stood him up and he said, *Good man. You're on your way. Now go back to Cleveland and start sobering up drunks.*

He only had a week's sobriety. *Go back to Cleveland and start sobering up drunks.* (You weren't an official, full-fledged member until you brought back somebody and then they got sober.) Clarence was a good salesman and he went back there talking to people right and left, because he wanted to hurry up and get somebody to go down to Akron with him. He was going to weekly meetings in the Williams' home, which is where the AAs in Akron were meeting with the Oxford people. Wonderful couple. (When you go out to Akron, that's on the tour—go by the Williams' home.)

Anyway, he's not getting anybody. The drunks are just listening; he's not closing any deals with these guys, and he runs across a guy with alcoholic paralysis. This is one of my favorite AA stories of all times. Alcohol paralysis is where you're lying on the ground and you can't move but you're conscious, so you can talk and people can talk to you, but you can't get away.

Clarence could work on closing the deal as long as he wanted to.

The guy couldn't get away. So, he knelt down by his side and said, *I'm telling you what you got to do. Do you want to get sober? I'm going to take you down to Akron.*

I don't want to. I don't want to do any of that. And Clarence just kept pressuring and pressuring, until finally the guy said, *OK.*

Clarence said, *Well, do you got $50?* It cost $50 to go through Dr. Bob's hospital. That is not bad for five days in the hospital.

He said, *No, I haven't got any money.* I mean who had money lying on skid row? *But my mother—if she knew that I was willing to go the hospital to recover from being a drunk, she would advance the $50 just like that.*

Clarence said, *Where does she live?* This was Clarence. He wasn't going to wait for him to get sober and go out there.

Where does your mother live? It was way out of town in the country. And he went and borrowed a car. He got somebody to loan him a car. He went right out there that same day and drove out and pretty soon the regular road ended. He was on a dirt road, and pretty soon that ended, and then it was kind of a trail. The hunting season was going on; people were shooting, and he was walking through the woods to some address out there. Finally he saw it.

It was a small farmhouse. He went up to the door and knocked, and this elderly woman came to answer it. He said, *Are you Mrs. Ryan?* (or whatever their name was).

She shook her head.

Ryan? Well, I'm here because your son is lying on the ground.

And she kept going, *I don't understand.* She was Polish and didn't speak English.

So, he found this man's mother but he could not communicate. She recognized her son's name, though. There was a young eight-year-old girl who was attending school and had learned English; she became the translator between the two and communicated the message. The mother gave him $50.

He went back and got this man to the hospital and he got sober. Clarence was AA's top Twelve-Stepper without a doubt. I mean, Dr. Bob had them all come to the hospital, but we're talking about going out and getting people and bringing them down. Clarence got into the automobile business, and he was such a top salesman, they gave him two demonstrators. There aren't many car dealers where the salesman gets one of each type of model to take home. But he did.

He used the two cars to ferry down the Cleveland contingent to the Akron meetings at the Williams' house. That's how many people he was getting sober.

Anyway, this went on for a year or so, and he noticed that almost everybody in the car was Roman Catholic. I don't know why he had so many Roman Catholics up there in Cleveland, but his carload was almost all Roman Catholics.

Something happened when the Roman Catholic guys got sober. Their churches noticed the difference, and the priest there would go up and go, *Pat, you look wonderful. What's going on?*

Oh Father, God is saving me. I found the Oxford Group down in Akron, a protestant organization.

This was definitely not approved by the Pope, and the priest would go, *Oh Pat, you really shouldn't be going there.*

But Father, it's saving my life. Then, pretty soon there would be two other guys and then three, and then the church would feel like it had a rebellion on its hands. They actually were calling these men in, saying if they kept going to the Oxford protestant organization, there was a chance they'd be excommunicated. Now that created a heck of dilemma, because both of those are terrible choices.

Clarence was thinking, as he drove down there, *What we need is a group outside of Oxford where we do the same thing. We'll just meet elsewhere. We'll call it something else, and that way these guys can keep getting sober.* So, he advanced the idea to Dr. Bob.

One day, Clarence was driving a woman named Abby home; she was the wife of one of the men in Clarence's car ferry to Akron. He was talking about how he wished he had a place where they could meet in Cleveland. Abby said, *Oh, you can use our house. It'll be perfect. It's a great big house. Our children are all gone, and besides, if you're meeting there, then when my husband gets out, he'll have no choice but to attend.*

Clarence tucked that away in the back of his head, and he went down there and he talked to Dr. Bob and he said, *You know, I got these Catholics, and they'll get excommunicated if they keep coming down here. So I'm thinking of starting a separate meeting up in Cleveland.*

Dr. Bob just went berserk, because he did not want to upset the Williamses and all the hospitality that they had. So he was caught in a tough place. He said, *No, no, no, no, no. Don't do that.*

Clarence went home and thought about it. He came back the next week and he said, *I know I'm not supposed to go against my sponsor, but I'm starting that thing. It's going to be Thursday night at this address.* Lo and behold, he did. The Akron contingent came up and tried to stop the meeting, but they weren't successful.

Here's the quirk in history that Clarence parlayed into a lot of controversy. The Big Book had come out, and the name Alcoholics Anonymous was now being used for the alcoholic squads that met separately. Bill Wilson would go to the Oxford Group in New York and then he had the drunks come over to his house for a separate little meeting, and that was starting to irritate the Oxford Groupers in New York. In Akron, they were not happy with that idea; Dr. Bob just didn't want to upset them.

Anyway, the book came out, so Clarence decided to call the group "Alcoholics Anonymous," after the Big Book. Technically, that was the first group to call itself Alcoholics Anonymous. If you were Clarence and wanted to use your ego and really stretch a point, you could later claim to be the founder of Alcoholics Anonymous … which Clarence did boldly, in the newspapers, with no anonymity.

He'd go on radio shows—*Tonight we are interviewing the founder of Alcoholics Anonymous, Clarence Snyder*—and this was not going over well in New York. But he was amazing. He wrote pamphlets on sponsorship and how to work with jails and institutions, and he started the first intergroup in Cleveland. His vision for the future of AA was that the major centers around the country would each do their own thing.

In other words, Cleveland would put together all their pamphlets and their telephone numbers and they would get the word out. Clarence thought the last thing we needed was some central office telling all of us what to do. You can see, there was some tension building.

The second level of tension was in New York. Even when I got sober in D.C., you would find the old-timers who would say, *Let me tell you the whole program. I can condense it down to two simple things: "Don't drink, and go to meetings."* That was the whole program. Don't drink, and go to meetings. Whereas for Clarence and others in Akron, it was, *Serve God, pray, help others.* It was totally spiritual, and New York was just, *Don't drink. What's the problem? If you don't drink, you can't get drunk. What's the problem?*

That tension exists today. I mean, in New York we'd like to make it more psychological. The last thing I've heard was that there are no groups left in New York that say the Lord's Prayer. *That reminds me too much of religion. We're going to get rid of that.* I think they say the Serenity Prayer. Then, out in Akron, *We got to go back to basics. We got to go back to basics. Back to basics.*

Between those two tensions, we got the wonderful middle ground known as our Twelve-Step program, and God as we understand Him,—it's a real blessing. It's nice to have that kind of tension because it will allow you to think about things from different perspectives, and it's still going on. I'm not taking sides. I love both perspectives. I think that's so healthy, and I really enjoy it.

Anyway, that's enough of the history for this chapter. I'm going to keep mentioning this. I started the discussion of our principles by going to the very end, the twelfth step, so that we see what the target is. It says, "Having had a spiritual awakening as a result of these steps…"

That's the only result that the twelve spiritual principles are aiming at—that spiritual awakening. Now, you hear, *Well, if you're just sober.* This isn't that. That's fine, but the deal here is to have that awakening yourself. It's a personal experience, and that's the jackpot.

When we go back and look at all these other steps—that's where they're pushing us. They're pushing us towards that moment in our lives that is the transforming experience. To be selected out of all humanity to have a shot at that is really an honor, because there aren't many groups that are shooting for that. There aren't many groups with meetings all over the place, with all of us sitting in there saying, *I'm going to do these…*

The only reason we're doing it is because alcohol's waiting out there. Nobody in here is a spiritual giant. We don't keep trying to do this stuff without being motivated. *I'm going to walk out there one day, and a bottle of vodka is going to appear and go, 'Hi,' and I'm going to pick it up and then I'm going to get beat up real bad and so that's why I'm going to do something I really don't believe in and I'm not inclined to even attempt.* And that's how we all got here and got forced into something that is the most wonderful thing that can happen to a human being.

I don't know why we're so lucky when it looks like we were so unlucky to get here. As I said earlier, when the cop pulled you over for a DWI, little did you know that that was God's man moving you towards salvation. He just didn't look too spiritual, but he was.

The last thing at the end of the third step was the third step prayer. I got this bookmark from the New Haven conference and I'm just going to read it to set the stage for the fourth step: "God, I offer myself to Thee—to build with me and do with me as Thou wilt. Relieve me of the bondage of self, that I may better do Thy will. Take away my difficulties, that victory over them may bear witness to those I would help of Thy power, Thy love, and Thy way of life. May I do Thy will always."

These are not thoughts that I would come to naturally in my

own selfish mind. You know what I'm thinking? I'm thinking, *I wish God would build with me so I can help others. I wish he'd just take me apart and put me back together, so I can help lots of people.* I don't ever remember thinking that, because I needed some money.

This stuff is not part of our makeup, OK? It just isn't, but the third step ends with this prayer. And just for the trivia crowd, the third step also ends with a prayer in the Twelve and Twelve. It's the only step that ends with two prayers: the Serenity Prayer and the Third Step Prayer.

Also for the trivia experts, the origin of AA adopting the Serenity Prayer was in 1941 when Ruth Hock (who typed the Big Book while working for stock certificates for the Works Publishing Company) was helping move the office to New York. They finally moved from New Jersey to New York in '41. They were getting inquiries from around the country—the book was selling, and it was starting to go a little bit. Her job was to answer correspondence. She opened a letter one day, and in it was simply a clipping out of a newspaper that an AA member had sent in. It was in an obituary for some man and at the end of it was the Serenity Prayer.

She looked at it and said, *Well, that's kind of interesting.* So, she started typing it on cards, just little cards. Then when she would respond to an inquiry, she'd drop a card in the envelope, so the Serenity Prayer, with no one knowing it except Ruth Hock, was slipping off to all different parts of the country, where they'd get the cards and say, *That is cool.* The next thing you know, it's part of Kansas, it's part of California, and all over the place.

Anyway, that brings us to the fourth step. I'm not going to go through the dynamics of the fourth step. I thought about this long and hard, and I want to talk about the big picture of the fourth step as I see it. Then, we'll talk about the dynamics of it.

I want to emphasize the big picture of the fourth step. It is not about admitting your sins and then doing penance for them. It's got nothing to do with that. That's the furthest thing from the fourth step that there is—making a searching and fearless moral inventory of ourselves. It has nothing to do with things we've done wrong that we're going to have to make good or that we're going to suffer and have to say twenty-five Hail Marys. That is not it at all.

The purpose of the fourth step is awakening to a brand new world, the one that your Creator made for you. That's what it's about. If awakening is the answer, then what's the problem? This is hard to understand sometimes. If awakening is the solution, then the problem is not realizing that we're not awake. We have no concept that there even is a problem.

We have no idea until we awaken that we were existing in a state of … not realizing that we weren't awake. We were following some reality that had been there all our lives and then as we worked the steps and this transformation took place, we looked around and thought, *You know, my family is actually a lot better than I thought they were.*

Well now you are awake to see how it really is, and so this is the state that we're in. The inventory is one of the most vital parts of achieving this awakening. It's so important that we have two steps devoted to it: four and ten. Inventory constitutes a sixth of our program. Do you ever think about that? It constitutes a sixth of the AA program.

So what's the deal? What's the big deal?

Here's the big deal. We have to undo everything we've ever learned about the world. Oh, I don't know about that. How's that for a big order? How about, *What an order. I can't go through with it. I'm going to undo.* That's what "old ideas availed us nothing" means.

What they're saying is we're trying to have an awakening and no longer see the material world from the old guidelines—but we're going to see it from an awakened perspective.

In order to better explain it, you have to tell a story. Why are stories important? Stories are the only way to talk about God, because nobody knows God. Nobody sees Him, but when we tell stories we go, *Oh yeah. I see. I understand that.* We see that at the AA meetings all the time when a speaker gets up there and tells their story. We see this marvelously intelligent sympathetic person standing there and then we hear the story of what a reprobate, hopeless piece of junk they were and we think, *How do they get from there to there?* And we realize, *God. There's no other way. I'm looking at God's work right in front of me.*

How did we see that? By them telling their story. Every time any one of you tells your story, you're telling a God story whether you know it or not—that's what's going to come across.

We are all like individual slide projectors and we project onto the big screen—planet Earth—the real big screen. This is the ultimate reality. We look up on the screen to see what's going on and we see all kinds of stuff, because society also has a projector going.

It's nothing more than a story that our ego is manufacturing inside of us, putting into a slide, and showing up there, and we go, *Oh jeez, look at that.* We've been told that the name of the game is *go up to the screen and rearrange things until it's suitable. Go up there where you see it's unfair and fix it.* You might go up there and see yourself in this little house. Then over there's a big house. What you want to do is change it so you're in the big house.

The secret of life is to go up and rearrange everything on the screen. The answer to everything is on the screen. That's where you look to see what's real and what needs to be done and what everything's all about.

There was a campaign slogan about twenty years ago, and they boiled it down to one line: "It's the economy, stupid." I would say to all of us, the line that we should learn is, "It's the projector, stupid." It's not what's on the screen. It's what's going on inside the projector. That's where we got to go. That's the ticket to everything.

Whoever told you to look up there didn't know what they were talking about. This is how spirituality works. We have to go inside the projector booth and see what is going on in there. We have to inventory the booth and see why everything up there is so upsetting. We go inside, and as we take an inventory, we find out that our ego is in charge of the show—it just resents everything.

Oh yeah, there is a resemblance up there. I can't stand it. No wonder I'm upset. Look at what's up there.

It's projecting these slides that we're making up ourselves. Bill wrote, "We create our own problems." That's how it's done. We make up a story or a slide, we project it on the screen, and then we react to it. And it becomes quite frightening.

So, I went in and I'm going to tell you what I saw. I went inside the projection booth, and the guy running the projector was Frank Morgan. Any trivia people know who Frank Morgan was? He was the actor that played the Wizard of Oz, and he was running my whole show. He was in there going, *Wooo! OK, watch out—bad witch coming in from one o'clock!*

If we remember the movie *The Wizard of Oz*, everybody was going nuts with all this stuff. Dragons and goblins and people are jumping out—and it's dangerous. Don't go here. Don't go there. Watch out for this. Watch out for that. Then they got up there and they looked around and they went, *Hey, who's that behind the screen?* The screen fell over and there was a little man standing there, and he went, *Whoops. I guess the game is up.* That's what we want to do to our ego. We want to expose the show until it says, *Whoops, the game is up.*

It's time to get out of Oz, and the fourth step is how it's done. That is where we go in order to transform everything. We go into the projection booth and we start correcting what's inside there— and we do that by carefully inventorying resentments and fears and sex. There's a carefully laid-out plan. This isn't being done to punish us for any wrongdoing or anything. It's going in there to transform what's going to be seen on the big screen.

Beautiful. What's really in store for us is beyond our wildest dreams. So, we need to understand this in order to be thorough. When I started doing that, I just went, *Oh God, all this stuff had to be fixed and I feel terrible and this and that.* I had no idea where it was leading me. I was thinking about a section in the Big Book: "Resentment is the number one offender. It destroys more alcoholics than anything else. From it stems all forms of spiritual disease."

It turns out we've been spiritually sick. Bill writes this interesting sentence: "When the spiritual malady is overcome, we're straightened out mentally and physically." When we fix the projector, what gets shown up there in the physical and material world is fixed. When we straighten out—the spiritual malady, the broken projector is overcome—we straighten out mentally and physically. Everything else straightens out—psychological problems, or whatever it is.

Later on, Bill says, "Our old plan was to get up on the screen and see what's wrong. I had to move this and that, but the more we fought and tried to have our own way, the worse matters got."

Does that describe the situation? Is that plan working, what we've been taught all our lives: *Go fix this. Go fix that*? No. It's got nothing to do with theory. It has to do with results.

How's your plan working? I see you're wearing a wristband from the nut ward. That was my sponsor talking. He also said, *If you write a book, don't put your picture on it.*

So we turn back to the list. Now listen to this, for it held the key to the future. The whole key to the future is in this list that we're going to fill out in our fourth step inventory.

We were prepared to look at it from an entirely different angle. I just gave you a new angle to look at. I made up a story to see what the book's talking about. We're going to look at all of that from a different angle. We began to see that the world wherein these people really dominated, and then it says, *Well, how do we escape?*

And I wrote in here, *From Oz? OK, I see the deal. I got to get out of here. Well, how do we get out of Oz?* We saw that these resentments must be mastered, but how? We could not wish them away any more than alcohol. How are we ever going to do this?

Here we go. We ask God to help us show them the same tolerance, pity, and patience that we would cheerfully give to a sick friend. At least, God will show us how to take a kindly and tolerant view of each and every one. God will help me have a tolerant and kindly view of everything. In other words, everything changes as a result of this kind of work.

I also sometimes sarcastically think, *Thanks a lot, society*, when I read the sentence, "Wasn't it because self-reliance failed us?" I don't know what you were taught, but I was taught self-reliance. You better rely on yourself. *If you can't trust yourself, who else are you going to trust? You have to do it, you're the man. Do it. You're the man. You're the woman. Do it. You're it. You're it. Go do it. Don't ask for help. You do it. Real man never asks for help. No, no, no, self-reliance.*

Boy, I'd like to find whoever's preaching that one. Perhaps there's a better way than self-reliance. You think there could be a better way than self-reliance? Let's see, self-reliance got me into the nut ward.

Hey, maybe there could be a better way.

We think so, for we are now on a different basis, a different perspective. It's a basis of trusting and relying upon God. We trust infinite God rather than our finite selves.

We are in the world to play the role that He assigns. How does He assign us the role? He puts a slide in the projector, it goes up there. We go, *Oh, I see what I have to be doing.* We will intuitively know how to handle situations that used to baffle us. Inventory is the adjustment of our spiritual self to transform everything else— including the big screen.

5

The Value of Being Wrong

I DIDN'T REALLY finish with Clarence Snyder. He was out in Cleveland and started an intergroup and wrote pamphlets on how to sponsor people. He was very forward thinking compared to the rest of the country. Cleveland had so many people sober that it was a natural target for the first convention because they knew they could get lots of people to come. As a matter of fact, they had the 10th Anniversary Conference of Alcoholics Anonymous in Cleveland –they got three thousand people to show up in 1945.

I'm sure that the main guy behind that was probably Clarence—*Let's get them all here to Cleveland!* Clarence's story in the Big Book is "The Brewmeister," and it was in the first two editions. He got the title for that, which hardly described his life, which was, as you heard, drinking whiskey and being out on the road with trucks and really just getting sick as a dog.

But way back when he first got married, and his wife had gotten pregnant, the doctor told Clarence that a glass of beer, once in a while, might be good for his wife. So being a good husband, he decided to set up his own brewery in the house and started with something pretty small—but there wouldn't be any left for her to have a glass. So he had to get a bigger container of home brew, and I don't know if she ever got a glass, but he got an awful lot of beer and started having parties in his town. That went on for a number of years, until he found that whiskey got you there a lot quicker and you didn't have to pour down 48 ounces of liquid. You could just use the beer as a chaser, and that became the thing for the future.

Clarence later moved to St. Petersburg, Florida. As the elder statesman in AA with the most time, he was in big demand to go around and speak, to do workshops, to do step studies and he did that year after year after year. Maybe about five or six years before he died, he met a lady, Grace. They got married and moved to Casselberry, Florida, and that's where he spent his final days.

The Florida retreats that he organized were really popular all over the country. People with long-term sobriety would come, especially from areas where spirituality wasn't emphasized as much as other areas. So there was this psychological approach up in New York and part of New England, and then there was the Christian approach out of Akron. So the Akron people that came through with that influence had a much heavier dose of spirituality and the steps.

The people who didn't have the heavy dose of spirituality were looking at the people who did, and they were going, *Why is that guy happier than I am? We both have twenty years, and we both have the same kind of income, and we both have a house and how is he walking around happy all the time? What the heck is going on?* That sort of led to, *Well, maybe I've got to dig a little deeper here and take my program to another level.* There would be new people who attended, but there were also lots of people who had some time in the program that went to Clarence's retreat.

Over the years it's been said that the retreats were religious, but they really weren't. He was very careful to divide them into two parts. There was the AA part, which stayed strictly with the literature; the steps. When that was over, participants could leave if they wanted because next, people would be saved by Jesus. But that was always part of Clarence's deal—he wouldn't back off, he wouldn't stop talking about that, and he wouldn't stop breaking his anonymity.

He said, *The traditions weren't around while I got sober, so why the hell should I care about them?* I don't know, but some of it may have been that the traditions came out of New York, and if you recall there was a tug of war between New York and Akron, so regardless he really made a wonderful contribution.

While I'm on this subject of New York and Akron—it was kind of funny that there was a series of coincidences. A very powerful guy in New York was Jim Burwell, who was a former atheist; he was very big in getting AA started there and then helped Fitz in Washington, D.C. and then Philadelphia.

So his influence was pretty strong, and he wasn't trying to make it a non-spiritual program. What he wanted was to fake out the new alcoholics by leading them to believing it was a psychological program. So we pushed the God stuff way down to the end, and then after we had them here for a while, then we'd tell them about the spirituality. His theory was that it would widen a net, get more people to come in, and in the long run, reach more alcoholics. Whether that's true or not, I have no idea, but that's the thinking behind it.

Meanwhile, the Oxford Group in New York was starting to get tired of the alcoholics. The Oxford Group in Akron didn't want them to leave, even as the inevitable became real—there were so many new alcoholics that the rest of the Oxford Groupers were feeling outnumbered. You know us alcoholics—we're recruiting, and we're out there finding more people to join. So Bill was holding little separate meetings in his home on Clinton Street in Brooklyn, and also they would meet at the cafeteria after the Oxford Group. The Oxford Group people, I don't know if they went home, but the alcoholics would all hang together and go out for coffee and a sandwich like we do today—must be something about being an alcoholic that after a meeting you have to go get some coffee and ice cream or something.

Anyway, the Oxford Group was trying to get the meetings at Bill's house and the cafeteria stopped, and they were putting a lot of pressure on the alcoholic members of the Oxford Group to stop going there. The term they used was, *You're not doing this 100 percent.* Whereas in Akron, it was very difficult for Dr. Bob to even consider leaving, because they had such dear friends in the Oxford Groups out there, especially the Williamses, who gave them their home to hold the meetings. So it really was all the way up into 1940 before they finally moved to Dr. Bob's house and then down to the King Street School, where there is still a meeting on Wednesday nights. If you go out to Akron, that's the meeting that came from Dr. Bob's house.

Now, in addition to those people, we very often hear about Sister Ignatia, a wonderful Catholic nun from Ireland, who was at the St. Thomas Hospital in Akron and was very interested in helping alcoholics. She had actually helped some before Dr. Bob got sober. She had another doctor who was smuggling them into the place where they sold flowers in the hospital. They put a cot in there and treated them there, because if the administration knew—

You got what in there?

A drunk.

We don't want drunks in the hospital. They throw up and bother the other patients. We can't have them in here.

She was their defender, and of course, when Dr. Bob came along, they were a natural pair to start this alcohol approach. She ended up creating a special place in Akron for alcoholics. It was a five-day deal, just like Dr. Bob. That's how long it took to dry out and get told about spirituality. The Oxford Group members would come visit the drunks.. As they were leaving, Sister Ignatia would call them in very privately and say, *I want to give you this sacred heart medallion.* This is a very Catholic thing, and it was made out of felt generally, with a little picture of a bleeding heart. She gave it to them to keep in their pocket, much like our coins today. It was the predecessor of keeping your good luck charm in your pocket.

She looked them right in the eye and she said, *If you are going to take a drink, you have to bring this back to me first.* And she said it in such a strong fashion that it was really hard for alcoholics to take that first drink with that thing in their pockets. *Damn. Sister Ignatia will find out about this, and she'll talk to the people up there, and I'll be in trouble no matter what happens.* Thousands of people, from all religions, got a sacred heart medallion.

Around 1950 or a little after, Dr. Bob died, and the Catholic Church transferred her to Cleveland, where she set up a very exact replica of what she had done in Akron. She named it Rosary Hall Solarium after Dr. Bob's initials, RHS, and did the same thing there with thousands of alcoholics. With the five days, she had a name for each day. Day of Reception; Day of Realization; Day of Moral Inventory; Day of Resolution; and Day of Plans for the Future. AA was there, and they got sponsors and all of that. She was a major contributor; she died in 1966.

One other person that I want to mention was a man who joined the Oxford Group up in Massachusetts in 1923, and his name was Jim Newton. While he was in the New York area, he became very good friends with Frank Buchman, who started the Oxford Group, and Sam Shoemaker, the minister of the church in New York where Bill went. Also with Rowland Hazard, who we talked about earlier, and another guy named Shep Cornell, who was one of the early guys and was also one of the people who got Ebby Thacher away from the judge and brought him into the Oxford Group. So Jim already knew some of the key players in AA, only he didn't know they were going to be key players. We find this throughout all AA history that there is this gathering or this accumulation of people like Bill and all the other people who were summering in Manchester, Vermont, because they knew each other as youngsters—the founder of Al-Anon and the co-founder of AA and Ebby and the whole nine yards.

Anyway, Newton was asked to move to Florida, to Fort Myers, and came to know Thomas Edison. He was a very good executive assistant, an organizer. Of course Edison hung around with all the big shots in America, and one of them was Harvey Firestone (of the Firestone rubber company out in Akron). Firestone was down in

Fort Myers and was talking and he said to Edison, *I need a special executive secretary. You know anyone who would be good for that?*

And Edison said, *Yeah, I have Jim here. He would be perfect.*

I guess there was a good pay raise, so Jim packed up his bag from Fort Myers and went out to Akron, Ohio. After he had been there a while, he made friends with Firestone's children. There were six children, and one of them, Bud Firestone, was a raging alcoholic. The father was doing everything he could to get him sober, and nothing was working. One time he sent him off to whatever hospital treatment they were doing back then, and Jim Newton went with them to see if he could help out. And on the way back, Bud was not doing well. He got drunk.

Jim said, *Why don't you come with me? I'm going to the Episcopal Conference, and I want you to meet some people.* And he was thinking of the fact that the Oxford Group had sobered up some alcoholics—maybe it would work for this guy.

Sam Shoemaker was at the convention, so they talked to him, and before Bud got back to Akron he was saved. Bud joined the Oxford Movement—they had to go elsewhere to go to meetings, but he did join. He got sober and was doing well, and his father saw this and said, *What happened to you?*

I got in the Oxford Group.

What's that?

Well, we don't have it here, but it's all over the place. It's really big, and it's helping people all over.

So his father said, *Well, let's bring it here.*

So phone calls were made to Frank Buchman, and it was planned as a major event. The newspapers were covering that the top dog is going to organize something at the Mayflower Hotel. Jim Newton had joined an Episcopal church there (the same one that the Firestones went to), and the minister, Reverend Walter Tunks whose name is all over our AA history, was asked to host the Oxford event. So into town comes the entourage, and there's an awful lot of publicity going out in Akron. *Come and attend one of these Oxford things!*

Firestone is all excited that this is going to be a wonderful thing for Akron. And attending that meeting, because of all the publicity, was Anne Smith, Henrietta Seiberling, and T. Henry and Clarace Williams, whose home was use for all the meetings.

Without Newton, the Oxford Group may have never gotten to Akron, and if it hadn't gotten to Akron, then Anne Smith wouldn't have been able to tell her husband about it, and Henrietta Seiberling wouldn't have been able to connect Dr. Bob, and Reverend Tunks (whose name was in the lobby of The Mayflower Hotel under the church directory) wouldn't have been called into play when Bill Wilson was sitting there thinking about having a drink. Bill looked over at that church directory and said, *Maybe I can find some alcoholic to help me.* He called up Reverend Tunks, and Reverend Tunks said, *Oh yeah, we can help you.*

He reached one guy, who got him in touch with Henrietta Seiberling, who then called Anne Smith and set a meeting with Bill, and then later on they all met in the Williamses' home. So you can just see that all the players came together when Firestone said, *We are going to have a big deal in Akron.* So Newton kind of played a very key role without realizing it in getting us started.

So that brings us pretty much through the '40s. World War II came along, and AAs stayed sober in great numbers; you see that in The Traditions when he's talking about the servicemen in Alaska and Solano beachhead. (They just had a thing on the History Channel about the Japanese invasion of the Aleutian Islands—that was the first time American territory had been occupied by foreigners, and it lasted a while. It was quite a deal getting them out of there.)

Moving back to the spirituality of this program and the frame of reference that I have been using –it's really been helpful to me to start at the end. What's this whole deal about it? Let me tell you the ending. People hate that when you go to a movie, but sometimes it can be useful in understanding what we are trying to accomplish as we move through all the steps. The ending is *having had a spiritual awakening as the results of these steps.* We try to carry this message about a spiritual awakening to the next person. There's a tremendous emphasis on this profound personality change called the spiritual awakening because it's in that transformation that it becomes easier to not drink. That is why AA is so successful. Because without alcohol, we have a way to see the world as a very friendly place to live, and I don't know about you all, but I did not see the world that way. That's why I drank.

The world was frightening. It made no sense. It made me see no purpose in life. I was a loner. I didn't know what people were up to. I just saw greed. *I guess you have to make a lot of money. I don't know what's going on. Give me a drink.* And then I found a place to live that was wonderful, and it was the world of three drinks, and in that place I was as happy as it could be. I wasn't wanting anything. It was just a lovely place to be. Unfortunately, I didn't stay at drink number three. I tried to improve on Nirvana and I ended up in jail. But I swore that the next night I would stay at the three level. Never could do that. And I know that I'm not the only one that tried. *Tonight I'm just going to stay at the three level.*

Anyway, when we take alcohol out of the equation, we're left feeling pretty bad, and we're going to stay this way. We don't drink a day at a time—and life is lived one day at a time—but our ego is telling us, *Yeah, but some of these people are thinking I'm staying sober forever. That's a long time to feel the way I do. How can I feel this way forever? I can't feel this way for another month. I'll be lucky to last.* So it's clear something has to be done about how we're feeling and what's going on inside of us. That's what the awakening is. That's the answer. Sometimes it happens quickly, sometimes slowly. Bill had a rapid one, and the rest of us have to be content with gradual change. But eventually, even ourselves we realize, *Wow, what they've been talking about is real. I can feel it inside.* And we each have our own connection with our Creator and that is what we maintain, or increase, in order to not go back to drinking.

So we talked about surrendering and coming to grips with the fact that we have a situation that only a source of spiritual power can address. So out of sheer necessity, we have to change our minds about Higher Power. Not because anybody proved it to us or showed us one. We were just shown the plain truth about our situation—hard cold facts. Unless there's a Higher Power, it's over. We didn't want to hear that. *Well, I'm not that bad. I'm not so bad I need a Higher Power. That's horrible to be that bad that you need a Higher Power.* Isn't it funny that we would think that way? *God, I hope I never need a Higher Power.* Then when we find out what happens we are so glad. But I didn't know what it was all about, and it seemed to me like that would be the last thing I want. The Higher Power coming in and messing around in my life—*How do I know what will happen?* My sponsor would point to the wristband from the nut ward and go, *Well, it may be better. I don't know.*

There was no winning with him because he would never talk theory, only results. I never could win. I was so far behind the power curve trying to earn money and come out ahead, and he just kept saying, *You just keep following the plan*, and I'm glad he did. We talked about how that inventory was so important that we had two steps for that. We used the projector story, and I've heard from others that they really found it helpful to view the inventory from a slide projector point of view.

Just reviewing that the way humans operate is to look out at the world and try to fulfill what's missing inside of them by rearranging what's out there. *Get some money away from that guy and move it towards me. Then I'll get a pilot's license and then I'll be up there so I'll move out of this into an airplane.* So we are moving, moving, and things kept getting in the way. *That guy got it, and this guy—what happened to this?* And then, *What the hell? Why was my insurance cancelled? You're ruining my plan!* Then I get up in the morning, I'm feeling halfway decent, and then I read the paper. Now I'm totally depressed because I'm hearing about all the things up there that are screwed up. I should not have read that damn thing.

So, we had no way of knowing that that isn't where the game can be won. That it is an inside job. We should have a clue from drinking that the game was an inside job. That you fix it inside here, and everything changes out there. So the point of inventorying is to take our focus away from the world as we see it, because what I'm seeing is what I'm putting together in my slide projector. I'm making lots of slides, and I'm putting them in there and then I'm looking up there, and I'm not liking what I see. Well, I made it. I'm the guy who put it together because these things are made by thinking. So whatever thoughts I'm thinking up, I'm seeing that. If I sit here, close my eyes, and think the world really sucks, I haven't had a break in ten years and then I open my eyes, what do I see? I see the world sucks and you didn't get a break for ten years. It's right there. It's clear as a bell. I can plan it out to everybody. *See that guy? He's got a break. He's doing all right. See that? See that? It's true.*

Now, the guy sitting next to me told himself, *Everything is really cool. I'm pretty happy with everything.* Then he looks up, same stuff. Then he says to me, *Isn't that great?*

I go, *What the hell are you talking about? That's not great. That's terrible.* I never saw the connection between what I was doing and thinking. Thinking, thinking, thinking, thinking, thinking. That is the obsession with every human being.

What are you going to do about it?

I'm going to think about it. I'm going to think about it.

How long do you think you're going to think about it?

Oh man, I don't know. It could be a couple of weeks. I got to think about this. I got to think about it.

So I go in my bedroom and stay up all night making about 2,000 slides so that I can keep looking at them. I realize things are worse than I thought—I have to think more. I have to think some more. Spirituality really is not about getting anything—it is about getting rid of stuff. It's about getting rid of everything that we created, which is our ideas. That's why Bill wrote, "Old ideas availed us nothing." Let's inventory all of them and get rid of them. So we have a plan for that, and it was laid out in the fourth step—how to categorize all the different ideas and emotions that we have, which are resentments, fear, sex drive, and the accompanying problems that come out of that according to us, because that's where all problems come from. Bill talked about our problems being of our own making.

So we have created inside a projection booth a million slides, and we just keep sticking them in and looking at them and saying, *Oh, Jesus. When is it ever going to straighten out?* And then we leave and go up to the thing that's trying to move it on the screen, and it will be like being at the movie trying to move something on the movie screen. *I'm tired of that guy always winning. Get off the screen.* You can't get them off up there. You can't affect anything up there. So now we finally say, *OK, let's go in here. Stop worrying about the world. Stop doing anything. Leave all the problems unattended.* This is the quickest way to solve them. Leave them all unattended. No one is even guarding them.

Some of us almost feel like if we are going to leave our problems alone, we need someone to watch over them. *What if they're gone when I come back to them?* This is true. If somehow we could work magic and take away all of the problems that everybody has in this room, who would you be? There would be a panic attack. *What would I think about? Nothing.* In other words, deep down there is part of us that is just terrified of getting rid of them all, because what would be left? Completely unknown, completely unknown. What would be there? That's what we are going to find out. That's what we are going to find out in this process of getting ourselves out of the way.

We say that we are a spiritual being having a human experience. What if we can get all this human energy out of the way? What do you suppose we would feel? What do you suppose we will then be seeing looking at the world? Would we, in fact, be seeing what we were supposed to see before we made up the big story that is our own drama? Before I made up the drama that I star in, you notice everyone in this room is the center of all your own problems, if they happen to you or not.

My closest friend loses a job. I go, *Man that's really rough but it's not a problem for me. That's his problem.* Anyway, we came to this idea—let's go inside. When I first took that inventory, I said, *Why am I doing this when I got stuff to do out there? I got to get some money. I can't be fooling around with this kind of stuff. This is time consuming. I got problems to think about. Filling out the sheet could take hours, and I don't have hours free from problem worrying.* So now you can see we are never going back to that. This is a new way of life. We are going to unlearn all the old ways that we saw things and that we lived. We are going to go inside of the slide projector and we are going to inventory all the stock that's in there, and we are going to throw out stuff that really would be inappropriate to keep.

As we make the list of the inventory in there, we notice that the word rationalization appears all over the place. *Rationalize, rationalize, rationalize, rationalize.* Now, if we rationalize a lot, do you think our inventory is any good at all? How do we know what we put down here as an honest appraisal of ourselves is of any value whatsoever? Maybe we should run all this by someone else. *Someone else? Run my life by someone else? What the hell are you talking about? I don't run my life by anybody else.*

So we have this fifth step. "Admitted it to God, to ourselves, and another human being the exact nature of our wrongs." As we get started with this Higher Power thing, sometimes it's not that uncomfortable to say, *Well, yeah. All right, God, this is this.* Then we say, *Well, He'll only notice anyway.* That's not really a difficult thing to do. *I think I'll make the fifth step a two-part thing. Admit to myself and to God the exact nature of my wrongs—that really seems sufficient.* But that isn't.

What is coming up here is one of the greatest principles in our program: it's impossible to see the truth about yourself alone. This is the step where, Bill writes, people of very high spiritual development insist on checking with others regarding the guidance they feel they may have gotten from their Creator. So if people of very high spiritual development always check with other people, maybe we really should.

And that's where our sponsor or whoever is going to help us with this project comes in. They are brought in to help us see as we bring up each slide or as you go through the list. We look at it and we go, *I have a resentment about this. Here is this thing. I can project it. This is what happens. See her? She's doing that, and this guy comes in, and then I'm the one who gets screwed. You can see it. It's right there. I had no part in that, right? You can see, and I can see it. It's clear as a bell.*

And the sponsor would say, *Well, no. You actually have four resentments to list as a result of your part in that.*

Why? I don't see it that way.

That's the point. *I don't see it that way.* And it's amazing as we go through each one of these slides and put it up there for our sponsor to see how he didn't see it the same way that I see it. He sees it from the big picture. He sees it in terms of everybody. I see it in terms of me. It's amazing how I only see how it might affect me. So we need another person to bring out the third dimension in all of this. In the beginning it's painful, because it means you're wrong. This is like the death knell to the ego. For an alcoholic to admit that he or she is wrong in the beginning when we first come to AA is like turning the Queen Mary around in Tampa Harbor over here. It's going to take about fifteen tugboats.

What are you doing?

I'm getting him to change his mind.

I remember telling my sponsor, *OK, OK. You're right.*

He said, *No, you're wrong.*

Bill, it's the same thing.

Well, say it.

I tell you that those words stuck in my throat. *I'm wrong.* Do you know how hard that was to say? *I'm wrong.*

I can't hear you.

Wrong.

You know what is so exciting now? If I find something I'm

wrong about and I can get rid of it. *Oh boy, I just found something that I am wrong about.* Gone. That's the tenth step. That's Chuck Chamberlain. Uncover, discover, discard. *Oh boy! Something else wrong. OK, gone.*

But in the beginning, it just shutters you to be wrong. I don't know about you, but it just killed me. *All right, we go through one item that I'm wrong about. I see your point. I did have a role, OK. I had a small role. I actually caused it. Now I have seen it, but I never would have seen that on my own. I'm glad that's over. Well, let's go to the next slide. You don't think that I can be wrong on this one too, do you? Well, let's put it up. That's the one with my father. Now you can see—my face is clear. My father was very unfair to me. I had no part in that, right, Bill? I caused that, too.*

It's just amazing. Now, in the beginning, you feel terrible. *I'm wrong, I'm wrong.* But every time you're wrong is like somebody pulled a thistle or a thorn out of your skin. Wrong, gone, and you start getting into it. Being wrong has some advantages. You feel better afterwards. *Wrong, wrong.* And then, I start looking where I might be wrong and what I have done. I'm starting to actually complete that inventory with a different perspective. It's good to see your part in it. It's great to try and understand them, and give them the benefit of the doubt. *Wow, I'm getting a new way of seeing things.* One item at a time. We're adjusting the picture, and each one seems like a painful little wrong. But slowly, we're moving these slides, throwing them out, and a new picture is coming in.

And as we will see as we get further along in the awakening, The Promises begin to be realized. We will talk about those. We see that The Promises accurately describe what it looks like when you finish this process. And as you finish it and see it upon the screen—*wow*—a major change in the world and the people who live in it, and a major change in you. Look, I never really would have seen the world this way, and I never would have seen people this way. There are a lot of nice people. As a matter of fact, there are a ton of nice people. Where were they hiding before? Well, they were reacting to me because my old view of things caused me to see them as competitors, as people who are in my way of getting what would make me happy. So the whole picture slowly gets changed to the point that we have the whole tail end of the program to maintain or improve that picture. Maintain or improve it. Maintain our spiritual condition out of the tenth step.

If we see suddenly all kinds of problems, where should we go to work on them? In the projection booth! We let them all go up there and go back at the projection booth and bring someone with us.

6

Shoot for Perfection

SEVERAL THINGS HAPPENED with Alcoholics Anonymous during
the 1940s. One was that they held a convention in Cleveland to
celebrate ten years. It was put on mostly by the people in Cleveland (and Clarence), and they got almost 2,500 to 3,000 people,
which is a lot. AA was only ten years old, and that many people
showed up—some from Canada—and it was a wonderful event. It
was amazing just to see the beginnings of what we now have at the
international level with 70,000 people.

If you're new, you want to keep track of these things—every
five years is the International Conference. The next will be 2015 in
Atlanta, 2020 in Detroit, and 2025 in Vancouver, BC. And they
will have rooms at local universities and bus transportations so you
don't have to get a fancy hotel downtown.

Also in the '40s, Rowland Hazard passed away. We mentioned
him earlier and what was kind of sad was that he lost two sons in
World War II, as did a lot of families in this country.

The Grapevine was started by six people in the New York office
who wanted to have a local newsletter that people could read, and
that has developed into a major publication of AA writings by
AA members sharing their thoughts on how their lives are going.
The main thing that happened during those years was Bill started
to work on the Traditions. This is in spite of him having terrible

depression. Not much was known about depression at that time.

You'll also see photographs of Dr. Harry Tiebout, who was the psychiatrist who was a big fan of AA and tried to help out wherever he could. Bill was seeing him to try and do something about his depression because it went on for quite a few years off and on. We've talked about the way news spreads around AA, and it wasn't long before AAs around the country were spreading the rumor that Bill wasn't working a very good program. *Why else would he be having depressions? Maybe he's been taking a few on the side and, for sure, he's taking pills.* He had to endure that in silence and just let it go.

So, if you've heard something about anything and it really wasn't founded—you heard Frank say it or you heard Louise say it—you just don't need to repeat it. It is amazing how that just goes all the way around and can cause a lot of confusion. That was a perfect example right there.

Those of you that are new, we have these Traditions. Bill saw the problems that were evolving once you get big. You don't have any problems that require traditions when you're small. It's when you get big and you're starting to have conflicts within the groups … then you're having conflicts between the groups … and then you're having conflicts between Cleveland and New York, and then between California and New York. So, Bill started looking at these, and as he travelled around the country, he would ask questions of people, and people were writing letters in to get advice about things. So, out of all of these, he started writing the Traditions in the middle of having those depressions, and they were adopted in 1950.

The first one has to do with unity. If we as individuals don't put the well-being of AA ahead of ourselves, there won't be any place to go. This is it; this is the last resort for us last-gaspers. And ironically, new people seem to sense this without even being told. They just kind of go, *You know, I'm a wise guy everywhere else, but I think I'll behave myself here at this AA meeting. It's just like because I need this, and it really is important.* And then we see everybody else who used to be wise guys and jokesters and everything. When the meeting starts, people are staying focused and putting the importance of the fellowship first. And certainly, no group takes more care of an individual than AA. It's one of the great spiritual things, which is to put something ahead of yourself. It is a great source of peace when we realize that the smaller we can make ourselves, the happier we're going to be.

The next one has to do with who's in charge. And the story they use in the Twelve in Twelve is a typical one. If AA is not in a certain little town somewhere, one guy or gal goes there and starts an AA meeting. That's how you'd get started; you just show up in Chicago with a Big Book and go find a doctor and say, *Are there any drunks around here? You've got two? Good! Tell them to come to my house on Monday night.*

So, now there is the My House group of alcoholics in Chicago. It officially started and totally run by the guy who started it, because it was in his house. And his particular meetings were at 7:45, because that was the earliest they could get home from work. Fifty years later, they're still meeting at 7:45. Why? *I don't know— we've always done it that way.*

He'd get them there and say, *OK, we're going to read the Big Book together, and then we're going to do this and this in the meeting. Now let's say a prayer, and that's it and we're closing up the meeting.* So, they told all the people and they were getting sober, and pretty soon there were fifteen people; two of them had to stand in his living room because that was all the room there was.

And they said to Joe, *Why don't we move it?*

No. It's my house; it's my meeting. We're going to stay here.

Well, you know what? I really like standing, but not all the time.

Well, that's too bad. You want to get sober, you got to go blah … blah … blah…

Well, the meeting got up to twenty people, and a small rebellion took place in the group. They announced they were moving, much to Joe's chagrin.

You are ungrateful drunks. After all I've done for you, you're moving.

We don't want to stand up, and I can't even fit in there. Everybody smelled of BO, it's terrible in there, Joe. We're going to a new place. And he had his choice now, because the group just decided.

There's no one in charge. The group just decided, and he had his choice of becoming an elder statesman or a bleeding deacon. And sometimes somebody like that will get bent out of shape and go out and get drunk. But if he was smart, he'd recognize, *Isn't it wonderful that these people I got sober are now taking responsibility for themselves and they're running the meeting? I ought to go there and watch it. This is pretty exciting. This is sobriety in action.* And so, there we have people with long-term sobriety available at all meetings but not running them. And they are there in case a problem arises.

So, if five years later the treasurer runs off with all the money, it shakes the group big time, but you can go to the old-timer and ask, *What did you do? The guy ran off with the money.*

Oh, don't worry about it; that happens all the time. We just take up another collection, and then you can be the treasurer. We calm everybody down and we move on.

And so, it is really spiritually guided by our loving Higher Power. And when we're really having a problem, we can all just sit and go, *Why don't we just pray for a minute and see what answer we come up with?* And so that's who's in charge of Alcoholics Anonymous.

Then we have the tradition about who can become a member. Every organization around the world has the membership requirements, forms to fill out, and all of that. Sociologists often wonder, *How does AA function? What are its membership requirements?* And of course, if you've been around a while you know the only requirement is the desire to stop drinking. So, this is possibly the only organization where you decide if you're a member. The organization has nothing to say about it. How do you like that for an organization?

Hello, I'm a member.

Well, who invited you in?

I did.

And it's wide-open to anybody. If you have a desire to stop drinking, you don't have to prove it. Now, let me assure you, we don't have many non-alcoholics just hanging around because it's such a cool place to be. You don't have social climbers putting "member of AA" on their resumes. But it's quite ironic that, in the beginning, they were very frightened that they could fall apart easily. It was brand new, and when they looked around, everybody they had there had arrived at AA almost dead.

Let's say they had been around a long, long time. What we call low-bottom long-term drinking drunks. They looked around and they said to themselves, *I guess this is the mold.* So, if somebody younger came in who still had a car, there was a great debate whether they should let them in. *Is this the right type of alcoholic?* They had a lot of fear about the membership in the beginning. And if you were having problems with other substances (or gambling or whatever it was), that was frightening.

I think we'd better limit ourselves. They (these early members) finally through talking to Bill decided to ask, *What would God do?*

When a person showed up and said, *I'm an alcoholic and I got a million other things wrong,* they said, *Come on in, the door's wide open. Do you have a desire to stop drinking? If you want to be a member, you're in.* So, you can see how amazingly loose things are.

You wonder, *Where does that discipline come from? Nobody's in charge? Nobody can tell anybody else to do anything? Where does this discipline come from?*

And, well, we all know the answer. It comes from alcohol; that's where it comes from. We don't need to tell people, *Well, you better do this or you better do that or that will happen; something bad does happen.* And so, it is as though, right around all AA groups are little half-pints of vodka, and they just patrol all around them in the bushes out there. They're just waiting for somebody to come out and go, *I'm tired of that place; I'm going to leave.*

And then they jump up: *Hey, over here!*

You say, *Look at that! It must be God's will…*

And then the vodka gets ahold of you and says, *I understand you're not willing to stay in AA.*

No, I'm not going to stay in there.

Well, we'll see about that—watch this.

And then, alcohol beats and beats and beats, and then you'll say, *Well, maybe I will go try AA.* So, you can see, discipline comes from the disease itself.

The next one has to do with the fact that any group can run its meetings anyway they want unless it affects the reputation of AA as a whole. But even if it does, nobody can do anything about it. You will get a letter from New York saying; *We think that just reading comic books at the meeting probably won't get everybody sober. We just want to let you know.*

There was a group in Richmond, Virginia that decided to serve beer at AA meetings. That did not go down well with the other groups in the area who believed that was wrong, that it would ruin AA. So, GSO in New York sent a letter saying, *We don't think it's a good idea to serve beer.* The thinking was that back in those days, everybody drank whiskey, and beer was the free chaser—wine or beer or ginger ale. So, they figured as long as you eliminate the whiskey, everyone would be fine. The problem was the members forgot where the meeting was and what night it met. So, the idea of serving beer at meetings fell under its own weight, and it didn't need anyone helping them. But this is how groups get so different; they can be an hour and a half long, you can have a speaker, take a break, come back and discuss it—it's strictly up to the group. And of course, we try not to do something that would embarrass AA.

Then we come to a very important tradition called "Primary Purpose." This is the tradition that reminds us that Alcoholics Anonymous has only one primary purpose: to help the next alcoholic. End of story. We do one thing extremely well. We can't do ten things without diluting everything. And so, many of us have other problems—I'm a golf addict, somebody else is a gambling addict, somebody else is a drug addict, an overeater... What is being suggested in AA is we just talk about alcohol and eliminate the others. If there's a brand-new person in the back of the room and I spend fifteen minutes talking about throwing up food in order to keep my weight down, he might not stay. There would not be the identification with the meeting.

The thing that holds AA together is one drunk talking to another. That's it. Everything else in AA is to support that activity of one drunk talking to another. Then we have the tradition that AA shouldn't lend its name to any outside enterprise because money would get involved or prestige would get involved. Way back when, I think it was Schenley Distillers who wanted to have AA endorse it as a safe whiskey. And then all the drinkers in the country would go, *Well, that's the safest whiskey to drink because AA says it's a good whiskey.* Treatment centers would like to say, *AA-approved*, but that's not possible. They can say they follow the AA principles but it's not an AA-approved treatment center. So, this is the main effect of that tradition.

Then there is tradition seven; we're fully self-supporting, and this is important because AA is such a popular and well-respected organization now.

A minister might come to another AA group and say, *How do I get one started in my church? I think it would help my parishioners a lot and I really like it.*

And they might say, *Well, there are some people looking for a place to meet. I will send them to see you.*

And he comes in and he's so anxious to have them come that he says, *Look! You can have the hall for nothing, and we'll supply the coffee.* Pretty tempting offer, isn't it, when you don't have any money at all? We want to turn that down. We want to establish a monthly rental; it does not have to be very much, but it has to be something. We are writing a check to that church and we're buying our own coffee and our own sugar and our own coffee cups. And that gives us the arms-length distance with everyone that we operate with.

Because three years later, after supplying free coffee and free room for three years, the minister comes to the group and he's having a hard time recruiting membership for the church. He wonders if he could make a little announcement at the meeting. It'll be kind of hard to turn him down if you've been freeloading. And you might just say, *OK, but make it quick.* But you know you're not supposed to be doing that.

So, then the minister says something about, *Well, we have a wonderful church here; you go to AA here, wouldn't you'd like it if…?* And all of a sudden, something is wrong. And that all came back to the tradition of AA being self-supporting through its own contributions, which also is a very spiritual principle. Let's not become dependent on anyone or anything else.

AA is non-professional. We have AA people working at treatment centers, we have AA people that can take jobs as advisors, but we do not carry the AA message one drunk to another for money. It's always done out of love. And that's why it works. How many times have you had someone come over to your house to talk to you and when they leave, you say to yourself, *What's the angle here? What's going on? Why would that guy take his whole afternoon to talk to me? There must be some money involved.* You can hardly believe that somebody would come over and do that. And so, that's the part where we always stay non-professional, in spite of Bill's idea of having paid missionaries.

Then a sociologist may come and ask AA, *Jeez! You're all over the world; you have these groups, everything is just amazing. What does AA's organization chart look like?*

And we'd refer him to our ninth tradition, which says, *AA as such should never be organized.* So, there's the secret to the organization. There's no bottom or top. There's no hierarchy. There are just service boards. *Hey, we need people to be in charge of the convention. We need people to help out who can take meetings to jails. Hey, we need people to go out and do talks about AA in Tampa so they can hear about it.* All service work. Nobody is in charge of anything, just jobs to be done—we get volunteers to do that. There's no one in AA that can tell another AA member what to do. It just doesn't exist.

This is one of my favorites; that the most opinionated people in the world can belong to an organization that has no opinion on anything. And you've got to admit that's cool. I might say, *I think AA should only endorse the Washington Redskins.* I don't think that's going to go over to well in this room. It would divide us, one against the entire room. So, any position and opinion on outside issues is very divisive, and it's not necessary, in spite of our desire. Every so often there'll be a new way to get sober, like Rational Recovery or like the psychologist back in the '60s from Canada. There's always something going on, and we'll read about it. You can hear the AA members say, *Well, that is not going to work.* Individually, we can do all that, but you'll never see a statement coming out of GSO (General Service Office).

I always tell this story about when I was still in Washington doing lobbying work; that's when Senator Harold Hughes pushed through the 1970 Hughes Act creating the National Institute on Alcohol Abuse and Alcoholism (NIAAA). Then everybody started paying attention to alcoholism. The Health and Human Services Committee on the Senate side was having hearings on whether to put warning labels on alcohol like on cigarettes. And they were looking for witnesses to come with expertise, and one of the staff members said, *I know who we've got to get—AA. Who would know more about warning labels on bottles than AA?*

So, they called AA, and they sent a guy, and he said, *Yes, what can I help you with?*

And the senator said, *What is your opinion on warning labels?*

He said, *We have no opinion whatsoever.* The letter's in the record: *We have no opinion.*

And the senator said, *I can't believe it; they don't have any opinion.*

And it was just amazing. *Sorry, we don't.*

Now, that doesn't mean that individuals can't have an opinion. I have one and I'm going to share it with you whether you'd agree with it or not. I think that this is one place where a warning label could do some good. The label should say, *Warning: This bottle may run out. You should consider buying two.* See, we don't have a drunk getting in his car at midnight driving all over looking for another bottle. So, it could do some good.

Our last two have to do with anonymity. This is a program of attraction and not promotion, and so we maintain anonymity; just first-name basis at the level of press, radio, and films. And isn't it amazing how AA grew all over the world without promoting itself? It simply did its work and allowed others to talk about it like Jack Alexander. Allowed others to spread the good news about AA. And now, there is hardly a country that doesn't have AA, all based on attraction rather than promotion. What a novel concept.

The early fear was that if you were breaking your anonymity in the newspapers and you're kind of well-known, if you got drunk, all the drunks would go, *I'm not going to join. Look, that guy got drunk. What good is AA?* So, that was the beginning. *Let's keep our names quiet.* As they did that, they saw a benefit that was totally unanticipated. It was of immense spiritual value to practice anonymity, to simply address yourself as Mary, the alcoholic. That is your total identity: *I am Mary the alcoholic. I'm Sandy, the alcoholic.* So, we took what used to be our identity, which we'd used to make ourselves more important, our BS resume—all these things that we are—that were supposed to make us a big shot—and then we see, it's all ego, it's all image. And we came in here and said, *Actually, I'm just another drunk.* And we felt so free to get rid of all that identity junk and just be another drunk. That's who we all are. You're just another drunk sitting at the meeting. Nothing special about anybody; we're just here to get sober. Anyway, those are our traditions.

And now I'm going to jump into the sixth step. Now, we've been using stories to talk about these various principles, and the one we've been using is to imagine that we're projectors and we've been looking at the screen up there, which is the world as we see it. And we see that there are all kinds of unfairness, there's injustice, there's just a lot of trouble out there as we look around. And we come in here and we find the source of all that trouble that you're looking at out there is really inside your slide projector. So, stop trying to go up there and move stuff around on the big screen—go inside the booth and get the slide straightened out. Because once you get straightened out inside, what appears up there is going to be quite different. That's why we don't inventory *them* anymore. That's why we inventory *me*, because we're going to fix that great big thing by fixing *me*. And we're going to go inside and see what's there.

So, that's what we did; we went through this and we even brought our sponsor into the booth and we saw all of these images that we have put together—all very self-centered opinions and judgments that we've put up there on a daily basis. We've been collecting them since we were little kids. And then our parents helped us collect them, and society helped us collect them. And we put all that stuff inside of ourselves, and that's how we've seen what's out there.

So, we come to this step; this step becomes a monumental step. It simply says we're entirely ready to have God remove our defects of character. It sounds very innocent. As a matter of fact, in the Big Book, it just asks us if we're willing. *Wouldn't it be nice to get rid of it? Yes, sure would. Good. Nice job.*

Now, I want to just look at New York and Akron and compare them. If you remember, Bill started out telling everybody about this spiritual awakening, and it wasn't working.

Dr. Silkworth said, *Bill, tell them about powerlessness; tell them about the disease that's going to kill you. And then they'll listen to you.*

So, he got the idea of, *We won't get in to the God thing till later on.*

That was big in New York, and he also did not have the same feeling about Christianity that Dr. Bob and the rest of them did in Akron. He would meet with different priests and Fulton Sheen and studied Catholicism, but he never could resolve the divinity of Jesus. Bill just debated that until he died. It wasn't as sudden as that out in Akron, where on your first day, you were taken up to the bedroom upstairs with three guys who'd go, *Do you believe in God? Get on your knees. Hey, we're going to pray. Nice job, son.* Done. And then, you'd be given the pamphlet of the Four Absolutes. And they still use it. [*The Four Absolutes: Absolute Honesty, Absolute Unselfishness, Absolute Love, Absolute Purity.—Ed.*]

Now, the word *Absolute* is pretty strong, isn't it? There's no slack; it's like reading Scott Peck. I'll never forget that—I picked his book up and I went, *Hey man, there's no wiggle room in here, Mr. Peck.* Absolute!

Bill looked at this and he went, *Absolute. Drunks won't come in; they're not going to listen to us. Come on in here, you absolutely...* So, he didn't include the Four Absolutes as part of it. However, when asked about the Four Absolutes, Bill said, *No, I didn't put them in because I knew it would keep away some people. But I've put them in steps six and seven. They're there."* Now, you won't find them until he wrote the Twelve and Twelve. You can look for them in the Big Book in that prayer in the seventh step, and you could maybe read between the lines. What that word *absolute* really means is *shoot for perfection.* They don't really let the cat out of the bag until step six in the Twelve and Twelve. And when you get through reading step six in the Twelve and Twelve, you'll feel like it was written by the author of the Four Absolutes, because suddenly the tone has changed from progress not perfection to progress *towards* perfection, and we suddenly are discussing perfection. And this, of course is, *Whoa! Jeez, I didn't think we were going to go that far; I wasn't going to take this seriously.* But that's exactly what he had in mind.

And so, what is perfection? You see, a lot of us get nervous with perfection; nobody could become perfect. But we have to remember we started this whole discussion backwards by going to the end of the Twelve Steps with awakening; having had a spiritual awakening as the result of these steps. So, perfection has to do with awakening. It's not something that we can achieve on our own by becoming better and better and trying harder and harder. It is being in the present. The present is the deal in AA. The now is what we are trying to learn how to live in. And the now, if you want to coin the phrase, is the wormhole to awakening. That's the only place that it's going to happen; it's when we're spending time in the present moment. Now, for people who sit around regretting the past and are terrified about the future, this is a foreign place to go to, the moment—the present moment.

Perfection is the natural condition. That's our natural condition; a baby comes to you, it's perfect. What ruins perfection is thinking; that ruins everything. Eden was perfect until somebody thought it was unfair that you couldn't eat the apple. It went from perfection to bad. *I can't stand this place.* And that was all done by thinking. Thinking becomes, in the spiritual world, a great liability. So, I was just thinking about this, and oddly enough, science and religion both deal with the past and the future; that's all they study. Science thinks they're very close to totally understanding everything. I am just making up a story that they're going to break through; I am going to give them the credit. I'm going to say that, as Bill writes in the Twelve and Twelve, man has been trying to get nature to disclose her secrets for a long time, and someday, science will uncover all these and we'll be living in the happiest world.

So, let's just for discussion purposes imagine that they have discovered everything. They finally go, *Here it is—we got the smallest particle, we've got quantum tied in with relativity. Jackpot!* There's nothing left that we don't know. Break out the champagne, and we'll toast our egos. Now, the question is: What are we going to do for the next 5,000 years with nothing to learn, to look forward to? You know, haven't we spent our whole life looking for the next milestone … you know, when I get promoted … when I finally get married?

Well, with nothing left to know, the only place to go is going to be the now. That will become the place to go. What is contained in the eternal now is what our whole program is leading us towards—an awakening of the now. We get glimpses of that from time to time. Well, you know what happened to me yesterday? I was paying attention, and then I just got lost in the moment. I was just totally transfixed by something and found myself just lost in the moment. But after a while, I got out of that and came back to the real world. Oddly enough, that was the real world, and we came back to the world with all our ideas and all our thinking.

And so, as we get the sixth step, we imagine asking our Higher Power to come into the booth and help us get rid of all the slides that we've ever accumulated in our life.

Have you ever gone into the attic with the intention of cleaning it out? That crap has been up there for fifteen years. There isn't room for anything. I'm going up, and out it goes. Do you remember that? And so you'd open the trunk. *Oh man, I forgot all about that. Now, I think I'll save that one.* And then, out of the whole attic, you'll come down with three envelopes and throw them out. Because it's too much of a part of us. It's too important to us to get rid of these things—*that's who I am, are all these ideas.* This is the thinking that's driving me crazy.

And so, were I or any of us to allow that cleaning-out to happen, it would be perfection, as Bill said in the sixth step; allowing all of those slides to be erased by our Higher Power would leave us with no opinions, no judgments, no plans for the future, no list of injustices that were done to us. I mean the entire record about me might be gone. Where would that leave me? As they say, it would be the hole in the doughnut. Who would I be if all of that were gone? What would be coming out of the projector if there were just blank slides? There would be nothing but white light.

You know how wonderful white light is? Light's the one thing that scientist don't understand. Einstein said if he could have lived fifty more years, he'd spend them just studying light. It's often used for the Creator. Light—when people have these personality changes, we'd see a light about them. And they seem lighter. And if you can imagine this light coming out as we turned and looked back wherever we go during the day, this light is shining on our world and is causing it to be different. And the world that we live in is transformed. And we haven't done anything except get everything out of the way.

This is a very tedious lecture, I know, about trying to say there's nothing to do except get rid of things; that there's nothing in the program to do except get rid of and let go of things. We got two inventory steps. When we get to ten, it's going to be, *What else am I wrong about? What else am I wrong about I can get rid of? Gone... gone... gone...* So, that's just the brief description of what the dynamics as I see them of the sixth step are to enable light to flow through us.

Now, it doesn't look like that, but it is. That's the point of the whole deal is to get ourselves out of the way. Now, what are slides made of? How do you make a slide? Thinking—that's the entire process for creating a slide. Thinking is our nemesis. And our sponsors—well, I'll give you an example.

Our sponsor will get us and they'll say, *Look, Paul; this is the fourth time in a row. You thought it through and came up with a stupid answer. You have faulty thinking ... your character defects get up there. It's faulty thinking. Do you understand?*

Yes, I guess I do.

But, what are you going to do about it?

I don't know, I guess I'll have to think about it.

Do you see how that works? In other words, there's nothing that isn't solved by thinking. Now, thinking is the gasoline that we pour on that smoking ember that would have gone out by itself shortly. That's what we do to a problem. *Well, there seems to be a little problem over here. Let me think about that for a minute. Actually, it's not a little problem; it's quite a large problem now that I've looked at it. And if I were to look at it, maybe in conjunction with a friend of mine, it might turn into reason for a possible assassination; that's how big this problem is. How did it get so big? I just thought about it all night. I just thought about it all night. The more I thought, the more I thought.*

So, thinking is a very interesting word. I remember a book called "The Power of Positive Thinking." It really caught on. Positive thinking. There are all kinds of positive thinking, but what the positive thinking is doing is changing the stuff on the screen. It can do it. You can brighten up little portions of it. But there's something much more powerful than positive thinking. It's called *not thinking*. It's so far above positive thinking that you can't believe it. And that's why we eventually get to meditation, and that's what letting go is. You don't take something in your hands and say, *Wow! Here's a terrible situation over here. I know what I'm going to do. I'm not going to think about it.* That is letting it go, so that it can unfold naturally. It can unfold naturally. Things are resolving themselves as we sit in here. We're afraid to leave our problems unattended. They might get away. And then you'd have nothing bothering you. Do you see how silly we are about problems, in creating them? It's the only thing that gives us some sort of an identity. And that's why anonymity was so powerful in coming in and stripping away your identity and reducing it down to *I'm just another drunk like all the other people in here.*

And so, if we get back to the line that we talked about in chapter three—Is God everything or nothing? And we think about it—God is everything. Everything there is, is God. Everything else was made up by mankind. In other words, somehow we have a whole bunch of things that exist in addition to our Higher Power; in other words, in addition to everything. I first realized that when I was trying to see where I fit into God. God is everything.

And Chuck Chamberlain did that in his book; he had everything and then he was over here with nothing. And somehow, I exist in addition to everything, and anybody who's in here knows what I'm talking about. Yes, there's everything, but there's also me. There's me and all my problems and all the stuff that's going on on the screen.

So, I know this is not a routine talk. I'm trying to get at what Bill was talking about when he took it up to perfection. It isn't just progress; it is progress towards perfection. It is progress towards awakening. And if we are at a certain level in this search and we settle for just staying there because it's pretty good, we're really missing out on something that Bill made very clear is available in this step.

7

Projecting the Light

I HAD SOME people tell me that they have never heard my story. They don't know who I am and might be wondering, *Who is this guy? Is he really an alcoholic?* So I do not have time to tell my stories, but I did bring a collection of mental slides and we will just run through them real quick and I think that at the end, you will have pictures worth a thousand words. So we will just imagine these together, and you will probably get a good idea of the type of guy that I am.

Click. Here is a shot of me before I became an alcoholic. Notice how well I stand up, how close people stand to me, and how clear and blue my eyes are.

Click. This is several years later. You will notice I am having quite a problem standing, and there is no one within twenty-five feet of me and my eyes are missing. This is very unusual that somebody would have a camera handy when you are having your first drink, but this is actually me taking my first drink. This is a shot of me losing my first drink. For those of you who are not alcoholics, when I say I lost the drink, I do not mean I do not know where it is. I mean I no longer have possession of it.

So moving ahead rather quickly—*click*—here is a shot of me throwing up in prep school. *Click.* Here is a shot of me throwing up at Yale. *Click.* Here is a shot of me after I became a fighter pilot in the Marine Corps throwing up in an oxygen mask. That is something you want to avoid if you can. A lot of you may not know, but the microphone is in the oxygen mask. Sometimes I would hear from the tower something like, "Fixing Lamb 5-3, this is Atsugi Tower—you are breaking up. Please repeat all after leaving 40,000 feet."

Click. This is 1957. This was the first time I ever had a brand new car, and this is me driving out of the lot in my brand new car.

Here I am picking up a hitchhiker in my brand new car.

Here is the hitchhiker sticking me up in my brand new car.

Here is the hitchhiker driving off in my brand new car.

Here is the shot of me hitchhiking.

Here is the shot of the hitchhiker picking me up in my brand new car. Luckily, she didn't recognize me.

OK, moving ahead real fast—*click*—here is a shot of my children and my wife turning their backs on me.

Here is the shot of my parents turning their backs on me.

Here is the shot of the Marine Corps turning its back on me.

Here is a shot of me having a grand mal seizure and ending up in the nut ward.

Here is the shot about six days later when I went completely wacko and they put me in this straightjacket. As you can see, they didn't have my size. I take a 42 long, and that is a 38 regular. When things go bad, they really go bad.

Click. This is after I got in Alcoholics Anonymous, and it's a shot of me eagerly working the steps with my sponsor. I don't know why, but he always kept his military pistol on the table while we were working the steps.

Click. This is ten years later. It is a shot of me smiling.

Click. Twenty years later, shot of me smiling. All the rest of the shots are just shots of me smiling. So there, I hope the slideshow gave you a little bit of an appreciation that I am really an alcoholic.

And now for a different history lesson. As the '40s came to an end, Anne Smith died. We always like to mention Anne, Dr.

Bob's wife, because she is given great credit by Bill and a lot of the old-timers for being the spiritual leader, who developed a lot of the readings, who just kept everybody on course. She was a very stabilizing influence on all of the early alcoholics.

Also, Jack Alexander of the *Saturday Evening Post* went back to AA nine years later and took a look and wrote a second article reporting the progress he found. He really did a wonderful job of showing all the pluses and some of the little problems that AA groups have, but again, it was remarkably positive publicity about AA, which is our program: attraction, not promotion. We let other people say all the good things about AA. We just help drunks. The rest just takes care of itself, which is kind of what a spiritual life is. We just do God's work, and He takes care of everything else. It is very hard to get to that point, because our ego doesn't want to be caught up on the picture, but certainly that article helped us to see that.

Dr. Silkworth passed away, and of course we talked about him earlier. He wrote "The Doctor's Opinion" in the Big Book and he was very crucial in Bill Wilson getting sober at the Towns Hospital.

The first General Service Conference in New York was held (1951); it was the first time they got AA organized as a whole. After the conference, Lois and a few other women went up to Stepping Stones, where the Wilsons lived, and made the plans that became the foundation of Al-Anon. As you can see, it was a very few people who were responsible for all these things that we have down to this day. In '53, the Twelve and Twelve was published.

I graduated from college that year. I think they were studying me, because that was the year that Yale University was studying alcoholism. They were the original university that was studying it, and then it went onto Rutgers University. I don't know where it is now, but that was the origin where they were just trying to get a handle on this. Dr. Jellinek (Assoc. Prof. of Applied Physiology at Yale 1941-1952: researched alcoholism) came along, and some people went to treatment in the old days. Remember the Jellinek Curve. You would go all the way to the bottom of the curve, and then you come to AA and you see yourself come all the way back up.

Then they had the 20th anniversary in St. Louis and they had 5,000 people. So you can see the increase in the numbers of our International Conventions. At the end of twenty years, we had 5,000, and in Toronto for the 70th anniversary, we had 40,000. You can see how much bigger AA is and how it continues to just blossom.

Then *AA Comes of Age* was published and also the second edition of the Big Book. I have the second edition. It came out in '55, and I came in in '64, so everybody was using the second edition then. The unique feature about the second edition was the reversible cover. You could take the cover off the book, and the back of it was the same color—blue. You could put that on, and nobody would know what you were reading as you are sitting on the bus. That was to protect people from knowing that we were in AA, in case that bothered us.

Also in '54, AA adopted the Circle and the Triangle. It appeared on all the pamphlets. It was the official symbol of AA, and for whatever reason, in 1994, they took it off. Still, we talk about the Circle and the Triangle as if it were still there.

OK, so that gets us through the '40s and '50s and leaves me plenty of time to get back to our discussion of the steps. As you know, we've been using one analogy to carry us through, and that is the slide projector. We came up with this because we've learned through bitter experience that it's impossible to achieve happiness by trying to control the world out there or the world on the screen if it were a projected slide. But that is what we were taught to do when we were little.

They said, *Take a look. You got to succeed in that world, and you've got to accomplish this and all that.* So our eyes and our focus were always out there to see what's going on, who is getting ahead of us—what the problem is. As a result, we saw lots of problems, because there were other people trying to get the same stuff we were trying to get because we were convinced that that was where happiness lay—in getting that screen arranged to suit ourselves.

We came into AA and we said, *Wait a minute. If you don't like what's up on the screen, why are you walking up to the screen trying to move all the images around? Why don't we come back into the projection booth and see if we can change the slides, and then see if the picture up there doesn't become more pleasing?* That was exactly what we were talking about as we inventoried in the fourth step. *What are all these slides that I kept projecting up there that caused me great fear, anxiety, anger, envy, lust … whatever it is?*

They are repeated all the time. Everybody has their own pet set of slides. Everybody has their own pet set of problems. In other words, somebody might worry all the time they're going to fall off a cliff. Nobody else is even remotely worried about something like that. They're worried about not having enough money or not getting as much attention as someone else does. We find that we repeat these stories and these slides that we started putting together when we were young, and we just keep playing them.

Well, there I am—not adequate, just like ten years ago.

Yup, there I am—not much, huh? There it is.

You come back in fifteen years. *Yeah, there I am, still a piece of crap. It's been that way since I was… I got to go up and fix that. I am going to go up and put some good clothes on that person. I am going to run up there and get the makeup done a little bit better. Well now, I'm this piece of crap with good makeup on.*

It hasn't changed anything, because we have to come back and see what's wrong with these slides. How are these slides made? They're made by thinking. All problems are created solely by thinking. That's how every problem we have is created—by thinking.

It is not that I got fired. That's an event. I didn't have anything to do about it, and it's not a problem because I will go look for another job. The problem is I'm very angry that I got fired because it's threatening me and I'm frightened. That's the problem. How did I get that problem? Oh, I just thought it up. I said, *I'm very frightened that I got fired.*

Did the boss come in and say, *You're fired and you're frightened*?

He didn't say that. He just said, *You're fired. We're cutting back, you know. We are not doing enough business.*

So, I, my slide maker (which is my ego), goes, *Yay! Here's the chance to generate some more trouble.* And I just start thinking about it. You know the pattern—we can make about fifteen slides out of that. *Well, I won't have any health insurance. When I get sick, I won't be able to afford the doctors, so any small sickness will soon turn into a big sickness. Probably get malnutrition—I can't afford food, and I will be slowly starving to death. I'll miss two payments on the mortgage, they take the house—I read the fine print in there. So now, I have malnutrition on the streets.* You haven't got home yet from being fired.

As you all know, we could go on forever over all kinds of events that happen. So the reason that we have sponsors and have these steps is to allow somebody else to see what's going on. They come into the booth and they go, *Wait a minute. All that happened is you've been fired. You made up all the rest of the stuff. We got to get rid of this. We are going to take this one out, this one out, this one out.*

That's the wonderful thing of not trying to see anything on our own. This is one of the great lessons of the fifth step—the truth about ourselves requires a third dimension. It was like when I was flying photo missions; we would take two pictures very close together of the same thing. It would be like 70 percent overlap. When they got the photos back, they could put them together, look in, and see the third dimension—they could measure how deep craters were, how deep trenches were, and how high something else was. That is what another person—in most cases, our sponsor—does. It puts things in perspective. We've learned this by inviting someone into the projection booth. We find out that the way to make the picture so that it is the most comfortable thing in the world is to remove all the slides. *All of the slides*, because they are simply my mind's reaction to all the events I've ever experienced. The events are not up there. It's my reaction to the events. It's not just the event, it's, *That's the most outrageous thing that ever happened to me!* It just happened. It wasn't outrageous to anyone else.

Spirituality occurs not by learning anything, but by unlearning, by undoing what we have put together that really isn't real. It's our entire existence of ideas, which we put inside ourselves, that were nothing more than reactions to something that happened. Then we created an entire story based on the reactions. In that world, which becomes just a show business world, there is no God. It gets very lonely. Authors have been writing about human loneliness since almost the beginning of time. How do you deal with the realization that, when you really cut through it all, you're all alone here?

Well, we're all alone because we made up a story that we're all alone. We're the only ones in it. It's just like a dream. Did you ever have a dream that you weren't in? And the same with these stories—all of the stories. If each one of us got up and shared all our slides, we would be the star of every slide, just like the ones I just showed you.

If we looked at all of your slides on the screen, you would go, *Oh yeah, that's the time I…* Maybe there are positive ones. *That's the time I scored a touchdown and everybody cheered!* So that all I want to do is go back and play that one slide. *There they are. They're still applauding.*

I know, but you're fifty-eight.

I know but I like playing that slide. It makes me feel wonderful to play that slide.

The sixth step discusses the possibility of getting rid of every slide—as the step says, "We're entirely ready to have God remove all these defects of character."

What is a character defect? It's the slide. It is a wrong story. It is not true. If we could ever become willing to have these slides erased, then, as we talked about last week, when we turn the projector on, the only thing that'll come out is pure white light, which is our true nature. That is our Creator shining through us, and when that light appears on the outside world, it illuminates the way it's supposed to be, and we see people in an entirely different manner. When they are bathed in that light, which is what you feel when you come to AA, I don't know what's going on here, but it feels good. You're feeling some of this spiritual energy. You're feeling concern from other people who seek nothing in return, and it makes you feel entirely different. We stop being self-centered alcoholics, which we've been all our lives, whose specialty is bringing out the worst in people, which we're all very good at.

When I was in the Marines, we had a plane with engine trouble. We landed it to get it fixed, and we spent about five days in some little peaceful town out in Iowa. I think that town is probably still recovering from that. They started fighting with each other, because we were able to bring out the worst in those people. We just—*Give me that! I don't understand! Come on, let me talk to the manager!* That's what's being played on the slide: *This place is unfair. They rip you off in here.*

Where did that slide come from? There's a bunch of people over here that think it's wonderful. *No, it's not. They rip you off.* Where did that come from? I don't know, but it's there. I can see it. I'm projecting it up there, so when I see a place that rips me off—which I created—then I emotionally react to it. *God, I am getting ripped off!* I ripped myself off, and then I said, *God I feel terrible about getting ripped off here.* It's just astounding the emotional reaction that we have to erroneous thoughts. That's why distrusting your feelings is a tough one in the spiritual world, but a lot of those are caused by our own thinking, which isn't true. That's why we run them by someone else:

I'm feeling this way.
Well, get rid of it. It's not true.
Oh, thank you.

Or our sponsors can say, *Well, now* that *I'd be concerned about.* That is why we never try to evaluate ourselves on our own. These are the great principles that come out of steps five, six, and seven. They are huge steps.

Now, when that light shines on people, it brings out the best in them. It brings out the very best in them. When you finish your day, you come home and you go, *God, I had a great day!* And we have no idea that we caused it. The light just runs through us, and people respond to it. That is what happens. Just a smile sometimes, and you'll see what happens in a dry cleaning place or something like that.

Hey, good day, thanks for your help. God, I always love coming in here.

Then they say, *Oh really? Well, I love working in this place.* See how powerful that is? The light itself is the solution.

Now the problem is becoming willing to let go of all the slides, because that wouldn't leave much of me. There would be really *no me*. It would just be like God talking through me, a damn little puppet. *Hi! I'm Sandy. God is talking through me. How are you all doing tonight?*

That would be terrible, right? Wrong. Wouldn't that be wonderful? We'd just be an instrument, and we'd see everything the way our Creator sees it. We wouldn't make up any stories about anything. We would just be—that would be the end of it. It's quite a struggle to become entirely willing to have all of these removed.

We talked about freedom and being slaves to so many things: alcohol, sex, drugs, gambling—you name it. Let's look at it like a person who was tied to a tree with ropes of varying length. Maybe there are fifteen ropes, and you finally get the first one loose, so now you can go three feet away from the tree. Well, you're freer than you were. And then you cut another—*Now I'm ten feet away. Well, I got the whole ten feet to walk around!* But until you get that last one cut, you're really not free. *I am more free than I used to be because I can walk 150 feet all around this tree!*—but there is still that one. We're going to try and surrender all the ropes that we created, but … *I got a death grip on it, and I am not letting it go. No, I'm not giving this up yet. I gave up drinking.*

My sponsor said, *You can't drink.*

OK. So, AA is a non-drinking organization.

Then, he said, *You know you're taking money at work—that is embezzling. You got to stop.*

Oh, you got to not drink and not embezzle? So there are two things you're doing here.

And then, if you're going to have a happy marriage, you're going to have to knock off the affairs.

Oh, so there are three things in AA! No embezzling, no drinking, no affairs. Then, it goes on and on and on until I've let go of everything. So in the same vein, if there is still one rope holding me from being free, if there's still one clenched fist holding me from being surrendered, I'm not turning my life over.

God, you got everything except these twelve. I'm going to hang on to these for a while. I am not throwing this little black book away. Maybe when I am eighty…

So the sixth step is talking about perfection. There is a story that C.S. Lewis came up with that I just think is wonderful. He's one of my favorite authors because he makes up stories. That's how he teaches. I've told this one a lot—it's about a little boy with a toothache.

He's in grammar school, on the baseball team. They're going into the championship, and the coach says, "Guys, we've discussed everything. There's nothing left, no more practice, nothing. Go home, eat a wonderful meal, and go to bed and get eight hours of sleep. If you get eight hours of sleep, we're going to beat them—guaranteed. That's all you guys need, just rest."

So, he goes home, tells his mother, has dinner and goes to bed. He falls sound asleep, and at about midnight, he wakes up with the beginning of a little toothache. He feels it and he says to himself, *If I call my mother, she'll bring two aspirin in. The aspirin will take away that little bit of pain that I have and I'll go right back to sleep.* But he doesn't call his mother. He decides to wait and see if it'll go away by itself, and he waits and he waits and he's feeling—*Oh, now it's getting a little stronger.* Now he is totally focused on feeling the tooth. He waits two hours and finally calls his mother; she gives him the aspirin. He goes to sleep and he gets up, but he missed about three hours of sleep. He makes three errors, and the team loses.

Why would he wait three hours before getting the aspirin? That has to do very much with step six.

The reason he didn't call is that he knew his mother, and he knew she would run right in and get him the aspirin and he could go back to sleep—but she wouldn't stop there. The next day, she would call the dentist for an appointment for him to go in to have this tooth looked at. The dentist would look at that tooth, but he would also look at all the other teeth, and if he found some other problems, there would be a series of appointments until he had perfect teeth. He didn't want perfect teeth. He just wanted two aspirin.

The only help that was available was perfect help, and if you notice who we're contacting in the sixth step, it's the supplier of perfect help: God. We're entirely willing to have God remove all the defects of character. You think He's going to remove them part way? He gets rid of ninety percent of lust? I think He's going to take the other ten. *That's going a little too far.* So, this is the beginning, as the Twelve and Twelve suggests, of a lifetime job of trying to get willing now.

Next, we come to the shortest step in the program: "Humbly asked Him to remove our shortcomings." If we look in the Big Book, the seventh step prayer reads, "My Creator, I am now willing that You should have all of me, good and bad." So, there it is: *all.* "I pray that You now remove from me every single defect of character which stands in the way of my usefulness to You and my fellows." Make no mistake about it, that's all of them.

I remember telling myself, *Well, the reason I'm still a complete ass in these other nine areas is because God doesn't want them to go yet. They are not in the way of my being useful.*

"Grant me strength, as I go out from here, to do Your bidding. Amen." We've now completed step seven until you read the Twelve and Twelve, which came out in 1953, which is quite a few years later. I think Bill realized that this indeed said it all. But it didn't say it strongly enough. As he'd realized elsewhere when he was working on the original six principles from the Oxford Group, it left some wiggle room. *Well, I am all done! This is it. Just take everything. Thank you! I'm on to step eight!*

So the Spirit was there. It was perfectly clear, but as you see when he writes the Twelve and Twelve, it is more than most people see. I think he saw an additional dimension as he put together the seventh step. It's totally about humility, and humility is a very misunderstood word. It is a word that has a hard time of it in our society.

You'll never see a car ad: *Buy this car! People will call you humble! You ought to hire him, really humble! Probably he would sell everybody.*

See that lineman over there? Look at him. Isn't he humble? We need more humble football players and then we'll really have a winning season.

Humble seems to mean wimpy and weak—at least that is what I thought it was. When I got here and my sponsor said, *Now you see this stuff?*

I said, *Yup.* "Humbly asked Him to remove our shortcomings."

OK, well, you know what the shortcomings are? They are the defects of character.

Yup.

OK. All you have to do is humbly ask God to remove them.

I said, *OK, yes, that's what I'm going to do.*

And he said, *Well, how are you going to do it? Before you do it, would you explain to me the difference between just regular asking and humbly asking? You know regular asking: "Hey guy, would you get rid of these?" Now, how do you humbly ask?*

And I thought to myself and I remembered a movie. I think it was "Going My Way" with Bing Crosby, and there was a nun in it. Every time you saw her, she was up in her room getting ready to pray, and the light shone on her face a certain way in the mirror, and I officially recorded that look as humble. So I thought, *If I get up in my room in front of the mirror and look into it like that—God, please take everything—then I would be humbly asking.* Now maybe you did a lot better.

I haven't seen too many papers on humility, longer than one sentence or so. So it is a word that isn't really understood, and we say, *Well, if you think you have it, it's gone.* You know, we have a lot of funny sayings about it. But let's look what Bill writes: "Humility is the foundation principle of all of our Twelve Steps." How about that?

"Without some degree of humility, no alcoholic can stay sober at all." So we must have had some humility when we came in here.

Then he goes on to say, "Unless we get more humility, we will never have a chance of becoming happy." Those are pretty big words, aren't they? No humility, no happiness. Wow!

"As long as we place self-reliance first, the genuine reliance upon a Higher Power was out of the question." The basic ingredient of all humility—a desire to seek and follow God's will for us—was missing. There is a lot of humility in joining AA and saying, *I can't stay sober on my own. I need help.*

In AA, they say, *Well, just admitting that you are an alcoholic isn't going to do it. You're going to have to go to lots of meetings in order to continue to live and stay sober.*

I don't want to go to meetings. I don't think I should have to do that. I like to do stuff all by myself.

No, you go to meetings.

All right, I'll go to meetings.

This is additional humility. We are making a statement: *I am powerless over all this.* And then they tell us to get a sponsor.

Why do I need a sponsor?

Because you can't rely on your thinking.

What? I am a genius. Whose thinking am I going to rely on?

Anybody but you who will move you ahead. Anybody but you.

Don't you think that is a huge chunk of humility, to rely on somebody else to do your thinking? We have a lot more humility than we realize. We are well on our way to erasing slides and becoming transparent so that this light can shine through us. Humility is the light. It is the absence of *me*. If I'm not there, everything shines through. I am the cloud between me and the sun. If I can get out of the way, things are going to be wonderful.

But we can get to a certain point where we're able to maintain a certain amount of sobriety and a certain level of semi-discomfort, and we call that success. Well, it is in the very beginning, but we don't want to go through the next fifteen or twenty years in forty percent of the pain we used to be in and call that a win. Don't settle for that. Keep going.

Humility, "make me an instrument of thy will." That summarizes it all right there.

Humility allows the light to flow through because there is no self to block it. "Of myself, I am nothing." The light does the work in the slide projector. *I am nothing. God does the work.* It's all let go and let God. Let go of what? Let go of all the clouds that are blocking the light. That's what we have to let go of. You are in the way of your life. Your story is in the way.

OK. Well, I think you're convincing me.

One more caveat, as the lawyers would say. I hate to break the news to you, but erasing slides hurts. Do you remember how humiliating it was to be an alcoholic and finally admit, *OK, I'm an alcoholic. So I was wrong. I am an alcoholic.*

The first time my sponsor wanted me to say, *I am wrong*, I said, *Yes, you're right.*

He said, *No, you say you're wrong.*

I don't want to say I'm wrong. Being wrong is painful.

Well, it turns out every one of those slides is wrong.

Yeah.

Are you ready to start scraping?

I don't know.

If we manage to become entirely willing, the process of

removing old ideas is quite painful—Bill writes on page 72 of the Twelve and Twelve, "For us, the process of gaining a new perspective was unbelievably painful." He certainly doesn't mince any words, does he? And we stick to it and clean a few slides, and we begin to feel peace of mind and serenity.

Then he writes on page 74, "Our eyes begin to open to the immense values which comes straight out of painful ego-puncturing." The tremendous value, which is more of the light, more peace of mind, more serenity is now flowing in because I was willing. *All right, we'll discuss gambling. All right, I got to change that. Oh God, I admit it's wrong. OK, I'm willing to have it gone.* That's what we do here. We slowly go through what is called pain but is later on called effort. We begin to realize that every time we experience this discomfort it makes us feel better later on, and we start changing the name from pain to effort. It's like the first time you go to the gym to work out when you're out of shape. After moving all those machines around, do you remember how you felt after you got home? Every muscle in the body felt like it was dying, and you thought, *Well, it takes a lot of pain to get in shape.*

But as you get in shape, you're glad that you took the pain. *All right, look at this! Hey, feeling better! Breathing! I like this.*

What do you like?

I like the fact that I went through that pain. But now, we don't call it pain.

We said, *Well, I got in shape and now I'm maintaining it. I think I'll even go further. I think I'll now try to run a marathon. I think I'll do this. I think I'll do that.* We suddenly see the immense value of what we once called suffering. Only we don't call it suffering anymore. Bill writes that there comes a time when we voluntarily get humiliated, instead of waiting for circumstances to rub our nose in it. We saw humility as something that was immensely desired.

So, the seventh step is fitting in with perfection, which came out of the sixth step. These are why you hear old-timers say the old folk song: *Well, what are you doing today? Six and seven, six and seven.* Chuck talked about in the tenth step, which is *uncovered, discovered, discard. What else am I wrong about? What other slide did I suddenly find that is ruining the view?* I don't blame the view being ruined on the outside world anymore. I don't go, *God my luck—of all those things, somebody put that up.* I say, *Oh, that came from me. I can fix it in here.* Call my sponsor—*How can I get that gone?* Ask that that be removed. It is totally a wonderful inside job.

I do a lot of writing to myself. I wrote, "I suddenly realized that I know a lot less than I used to know about fifteen years ago, and of what I still think I know, I'm much less certain about it. And I think it's a step in the right direction. It's a step away from thinking that knowing is going to solve things."

In the military, we had the "need to know": *This document is available on a need-to-know basis only.* Then, there was, *Well are you on the need-to-know list?*

No.

You can't read it!

So then, we all wanted to be on the need-to-know list. You know, with these freaking cell phones, if somebody finds something out thirteen seconds ahead of you, you go, *How come I wasn't told before that other guy? I want to be the first one to know what restaurant we're all going to go to. I don't want somebody else to know.*

So, there is this knowledge, which is fine when you're trying to run a business and all those things, but in the spiritual world, it has nothing to do with being happy. Knowing and trying to know more doesn't help at all. What is comfortable is to be happy with not knowing and realize there isn't anything to know. There's just the light. So I can be absolutely comfortable with not knowing. They say the greatest source of happiness is getting rid of the need to know or wanting. That's the same as getting everything. It's the spiritual flipside of getting everything. It's not wanting anything. You're 100 percent happy. You've solved the equation.

Spiritual teachers don't really teach us anything. They remind us of things that we forgot, that were already deep inside of us. We were born with of all our own truths, and as we go to meetings and we hear somebody say something and we resonate with it, it's because it's reawakening a truth inside of us. I think, *You know, I already knew that somehow.*

So actually in the slide booth, we came in with all the truths we'd ever need (the white lights) and then we made up additional truths, which was our story. Well, there's the truth, which came from my Creator, and then there's the stuff I added on—and that stuff became quite scary, and it also became reality. That's where I live, that's where I spent my whole time. And that's what the twelfth step is talking about: awakening. That's why when I started this whole thing, I started with the twelfth step; the point of the whole program is awakening.

Awakening means we're now in touch again with all these truths that were there to start with. People who have totally awakened—you know, the Dalai Lama and others—their reaction that they have is, *How could I have forgotten all this? My God, I can't believe I forgot all this.* We didn't forget it. We went out and created reactions to events, and then we lived in the reactions and that became home, and it's a scary place to be. It's very lonely in there because you are the only one that made the story up.

8

Forgiveness

SPIRITUALITY IS BEING able to have the power to see things differently so that you really enjoy the world that you're in and could have enjoyed all along had you been able to see it correctly. We have a tendency to only see problems through our problem-making eyes and our problem-making mind, which doesn't enable us to see how wonderful everything, really is. Stories help us see through things.

There was a lady who came into the New York office in the mid-'40s named Nell Wing, who became Bill's secretary until he died. She stayed on even longer and finally retired [*after 36 years –Ed.*] out of the New York office. She was our first archivist. She put together the wonderful collection that they have up in New York: all the old newspaper stories of first editions and all of the Grapevines and photographs of all the big conventions. It's really worth going to visit. After she retired, she came down to Washington DC, where I lived, and it was really fun to have her give a talk on the Traditions, because she typed them. She was there working with Bill putting them together and watching him agonize over, *Well, I don't know if this would be good...*, and so she had a lot of little stories. She passed away recently [*in February 2007 –Ed.*]; there was a big obituary column talking about all the work that she had done.

The other thing that occurred in the '40s was the first Hollywood movie was made about the hopelessness of alcoholism called "The Lost Weekend" with Ray Milland; back when movies were in black and white. In that movie, he had the DTs and convulsions and the whole thing, and there was a joke in Alcoholics Anonymous that if an alcoholic saw that movie, he would swear off movies, because it would ruin his drinking.

Then in the '50s, Bill finally finished "AA Comes of Age," our first history book. It's a little tedious compared to "Pass It On," "Dr. Bob and The Good Oldtimers" or Ernest Kurtz's "Not God," but it was the first accounting where he went through his recollection of our history—it has pictures, photographs, etc.

Now, the other thing that took place in the '50s that needs to be understood—because we talk about this as if we really knew—is Bill Wilson and LSD. We hear these stories all over the place, so let me tell you what happened.

There were two doctors in Canada who had read about LSD being discovered in Switzerland, and some of the doctors there were having some success with schizophrenics in helping them see things more clearly.

The symptoms were kind of shocking, and it reminded the doctors of the delirium tremens, which are very scary. We don't get them that often, but I had them, and they were terrifying. The original plan was, *Maybe if we gave some of this to alcoholics, it would scare them so much they would quit drinking.* Well, it turns out that's not what happens, and the experience is an actual shattering or punching through of the ego, allowing the actual spiritual experience to take place. Aldous Huxley knew Bill Wilson very well and he suggested that they consider this for the alcoholics who were not coming into AA—not for the alcoholics who are already in. He thought maybe if the resistant alcoholics saw what a spiritual experience was like, they would come in.

We forget that we're just concerned in here with the alcoholics who get here, but a very small percentage get here. There's a whole bunch that don't get to come here. So it was taken in a very controlled environment. Lois Wilson took some, Father Dowling (Catholic Priest and spiritual advisor to Bill) took some, Sam Shoemaker took some, and as it was done in an extremely controlled fashion, there were no ill effects.

It looked promising, and of course, Bill didn't keep anything a secret. He's not like a lot of us. He just announced to the whole AA world, *I'm going out, and I'm going to try LSD.* And of course, that just opened up the gossip mill. *Well, he's totally depressed and he's going to get high on drugs.*

He hadn't even gone there yet. *There's his depression—he's going to get high on drugs.* But he wanted to evaluate it and did so several times. Don't laugh—he didn't do it for his own personal enjoyment. He really wanted to either include it or not include it, and he decided that it wouldn't be a good idea.

We're all familiar with what happened after it left the controlled environment; Timothy Leary came along and it was just handed out, and there were entirely different experiences. Timothy Leary wanted Bill to come up and to experiment, but he never did anything with Timothy Leary.

That gets us to the '60s. In 1960, Bill turned down Time Magazine's offer to put him on the cover; he had done so much for the country, and they wanted to recognize him. If you've studied Bill Wilson's personality, this was hard to do. (Dr. Bob would have turned it down in a heartbeat.) Then they said, *Well, maybe we could have you turning sideways, so they couldn't really make you out.* He just totally rejected it, because it would set a precedent, and other alcoholics would be suddenly putting "almost" their face on the front of the papers. They did a story without his picture on the cover.

Father Dowling died in April 1960, and AA celebrated twenty-five years in Long Beach; they had 10,000 people show up. Then in August '61, the founder of the Oxford Group, Frank Buchman, died. Of course, that went from the biggest thing in the world down to something very small called Moral Re-Armament, and it really fell out of favor due to his talking favorably about Hitler at one point. He regretted that later on when we all found out what Hitler really had in mind.

Then came the Carl Jung letter exchange with Bill Wilson, which took place in 1961. These are very important parts of AA history that are reprinted in the Grapevine all the time. It started with Bill's letter to Dr. Jung and Dr. Jung's letter back to Bill—and then about three months later, Dr. Jung died. It was very fortunate that this exchange took place when it did. Bill wanted to thank Dr. Jung for being a key player in starting AA, because, as we talked about in our first lesson on the history, a businessman named Rowland Hazard, who was an alcoholic, went to see Dr. Jung with the hopes that he could fix him. After a year, he sent him away, Rowland got drunk again, and he came back. Dr. Jung, the world's greatest psychiatrist, told him there was nothing he could do for him, which induced total hopelessness, which is a big plus in dealing with alcoholics.

In that state of hopelessness, when Dr. Jung suggested that Rowland Hazard try to find a spiritual awakening (which had helped some people recover from alcoholism), he went to the Oxford Group and in turn rescued Ebby Thatcher and got him sober, who in turn got Bill sober.

Bill wanted to write to him and tell him that this chain of events took place. He briefly described Rowland Hazard and the results: *AA is this big, it's in so many countries, we have this many miracles and you played a large part in it.*

Dr. Jung wrote back and he said, *No, I didn't know what happened to Mr. Hazard. I'm so glad that he did and I was trying to induce in him psychiatrically the equivalent of a spiritual awakening, because I always understood, after studying alcoholics long and hard, that what they really have is a thirst for is a spiritual awakening. They all sense there's something missing inside of them, and alcohol appears to fix it. It looks like a natural match, that it takes that empty hole and fills it with alcohol. That's why I sent Rowland off to have this spiritual awakening.*

Then he went on to say something that was pretty interesting. He made an observation about human beings in general because he had studied all types of human beings for somewhere around 60 years, and this is what he said. It had nothing to do with AA, but it does.

He said that human beings come here to this planet, and they have to deal with evil—we would call it character defects—and they always lose. *Mankind just ain't going to make it. The universe is too cruel. The only exceptions are people who have spiritual awakenings and are in a society that helps them maintain that awakening*—and that's us. When I read that, I just realized how lucky we are to have this terrible disease and be forced in here to have something that is one of the most precious experiences that mankind has—to see life and to make sense out of it, find a purpose and feel inside of ourselves the part of the universe that we really are.

In '62, the movie "Days of Wine and Roses" came out. Sam Shoemaker, the minister at the Calvary Church in Washington where the Oxford Group met, passed away. These were all key players in the starting of AA, and now thirty years later, we're losing them all.

The only major event that happened in 1964 was that three guys in Washington D.C. got sober. They were called the Class of '64, and I'm the last one—the other two have passed away. (That is being kept out of the history books.) I'm giving you unofficial information that will probably never make the history books, but that did take place.

In 1965, the same two doctors who got Bill interested in LSD made another discovery that would be extremely helpful to alcoholics. Almost all alcoholics had hypoglycemia, and the solution they discovered was called Vitamin B3, niacin. Now that, I remember because all of a sudden the buzz.

Bill Wilson said alcoholics should take Vitamin B3. Everybody went to the health food store. There wasn't anything like, *Well, what is that?* That didn't matter. Bill Wilson said to take Vitamin B3, so—*Bzz!*—everybody's down there. Now, if you take niacin instead of niacinamide, your face gets all blotchy red, and you kind of hyperventilate for a while.

There were a number of months where if you went to an AA meeting, it looked like everybody had a slip. I have no idea whether it helped, but Bill was absolutely sold on it. When he got his teeth into something, he wasn't going to let it go. He would write letters everywhere to all the different states just to get the word out. He set up a thing so people could write in and find out about it, and later on in the General Service Conference, they passed a resolution that Bill couldn't receive mail about Vitamin B3 through AA. He had to set up a separate post office box because that would be an opinion on an outside issue.

Then there was the conference in Toronto, which would be the thirtieth anniversary. Out of that conference came something that many of us found hard to understand: *I am responsible. When anyone, anywhere, reaches out for help, I want the hand of AA always to be there. And for that: I am responsible.* The feeling that some of us had was, *Is everybody acting irresponsibly now?*

Are we sitting in meetings, seeing a newcomer and saying, *Let none of us go help him?* Did this need to be said? It just seemed like announcing after fifty years that the new AA policy was officially "Don't drink." That's how it appeared to a lot of us. *Of course, if the phone rings, you go! What's the deal? What is this?*

Well, there was more to it than meets the eye. If you recall in the Twelve and Twelve, in step twelve, Bill had this little paragraph where he said, *We went out and asked psychologists and people in the outside world to take a look at us, now that we've been around quite a few years and are reaching maturity and to evaluate us quite frankly.* If you read that paragraph, it says, "These distinguished men had the nerve to say that most alcoholics under investigation were still childish, emotionally sensitive and grandiose."

Now Dr. Tiebout was from High Watch (recovery center) and he had gotten Marty Mann (first woman to get sober) into AA. He was a close friend and great supporter of Bill's. But as he evaluated, he would just write to Bill and go, *Not grown up yet.* Other psychologists would voluntarily send in or write articles saying they had taken a look at AA, and AA had a long way to go to become a grown-up.

If you're having problems making people believe that you're grown-up and responsible at your big convention, you announce, *I am responsible.* It's hard to believe that that was one of the big pushes in doing that, but it was so important to Bill that the outside world saw us as grown-ups. I don't know if it's ever going to happen, to tell you the truth, that people will say, *Yeah, I know lot of AA members—they're very mature and grown-up.* I think we are responsible, I think we do meet our responsibilities and carry on in society and achieve success, but if they watched us in heavy traffic or sent us a letter saying, "You're really not the best in the world" (which we would take as total rejection), they would find that we still have a way's to go on this hike.

In 1966, Bill's sponsor Ebby passed away, Dr. Tiebout passed away, and Sister Ignatia passed away. As the '60s are finishing out, there are very few of the original people except for Bill. Dr. Bob and Hank Parkhurst had passed away, and a lot of the key players and then all of the supporting outside people.

In 1971, Bill passed away. It was very important to him that they completely transfer all responsibility for the wellbeing of Alcoholics Anonymous to the fellowship and the General Service Conference. He had the hardest time from the mid-'50s up until he died separating himself from the fellowship as a co-founder and just being a regular AA member. He couldn't just go to a meeting and go, *Hi, I'm Bill.* They would all run over. He was the co-founder, and it would be so much pressure that he stopped taking speaking engagements and just spent a lot of time studying and writing at Stepping Stones.

OK, that's an update on the history, and now let's go into step eight. We talked a lot about humility in the last chapter. We have a tendency to make jokes about it as if it would be a bad thing to say that we are humble. Let's look at some examples of practicing humility that everyone in this room does all of the time.

You go to meetings in order to stay sober rather than trying to stay sober on your own. That is a total act of humility, saying *I can't do this.*

I call my sponsor up for advice—that's total humility. That is saying, *I can't run my life on my own,* which our pride would tell us we can. We're self-sufficient. So we read AA literature looking for help in living our own lives. The more actions that we take that show we can't handle it on our own, that's the essence of humility. That all leads up to, *Of myself, I'm nothing. My Higher Power is everything.*

Every step we take towards getting more help and turning more things over is pure humility. Everyone in this room can say very comfortably, *I get tremendous benefits from humility.* You would all be telling the truth—you get immense benefits from humility. That's what we're supposed to learn from this step: stop trying to solve things on your own and ask for help, which is the essence of humility. It is the crushing of the pride and the ego and saying, *There's no way I can manage this on my own.*

The eighth step is, "Made a list of all the people we had harmed and became willing to make amends to them all." We're continuing with our slide projector and our slides as an analogy to describe each one of the steps. We're now going to get out the slides of how we harm people.

We're going to take a look at this—got a little slide for gossiping, a little slide for being unfaithful, a little slide for anger, a little slide for self-pity. *Look at poor me, poor me.* Then we inflict that on everybody out there and we may wonder why they don't treat us well.

This is another step that is very brief in the Big Book. It's just about eight sentences, and it simply says, We already made this list when we took the fourth step—now we want to develop a willingness to go out and make amends for any harm that we've done. Then in the ninth step, it goes on to discuss how these amends are made and how to approach certain people. But there's no real discussion of the list itself and what harm is. *What do you mean by harm? We harmed people?* As you look to the Twelve and Twelve, you see a big insight into step eight. You see six, seven and eight are really quite powerful in the Twelve and Twelve. Nine and ten are dynamite in both books.

But for six, seven and eight, I've always felt it extremely helpful to study the Twelve and Twelve. Right off the bat, we find out about forgiveness. This becomes the lead way of approaching this particular chore, the slides where we harm people.

Without forgiveness, we look at these and conclude that it's partially their fault. *I know I acted terribly, but they made me do it! If they didn't do that, I never would have dumped all the beer all over their living room!* We're transferring responsibility for our own actions to other people, which was our specialty before we got to AA.

Bill suggests that as we take the fourth step, we also look more closely at harm and forgiveness. We go back as far as we can think, to when we were children, because not only do we want to go make the amends, we want to change the slide so that we don't do it anymore. That allows us to have an entirely different view up there in the future. Forgiveness is almost like a magic spot remover; just the act itself starts letting light through these various incidences, because it takes a lot of the anger that we have over the event and reduces it.

So what is harm? Bill described it as *instincts in collision*. The world is made up of people who are trying to go get something that's going to make them happy, and they get in each other's way. There are great confrontations taking place all the time, because none of us have used the spiritual tools to see we already have everything we need, we don't have to go out after anything—which will come out of an awakening. That causes us to live in complete absence of harmony with the fellow inhabitants of this planet. As we live in disagreement with people, we end up doing something that alcoholics are specialists in: bringing out the worst in everyone.

We just seem to have that knack. *I've never seen that neighbor so mad till you came over here! I didn't know he could get that mad!* That's not just when we're drinking; this is our self-centeredness before we get rolling on changing. As we have these slides that bring out the worst in people, we look up and see we live in a rotten world filled with people who are just at odds with us all the time.

Little did I know that I was the reason they were behaving so rottenly. I tell this story every time I'm on this particular principle to show you the point. My sister now has thirty years in AA up in Connecticut, and back when she had about fifteen years, my parents had their fiftieth wedding anniversary. She was arranging a party up there and was going over the guest list with me.

She went down the list, and she got to one uncle. I said, *Do we have to invite him, too? He's so obnoxious. We have this wonderful event and then—bingo!—he comes in and spoils it. Our parents deserve better.*

My sister said, *He only does that when you're around. He's a great guy—everybody loves him.*

If I wasn't in AA and she wasn't in AA, I never would have believed her. *I know me! I know I wouldn't do something like that! I don't misread people that badly!* But since she was, I said, *OK. Maybe.* Then I said the words that we all hate to say: *Maybe I'm wrong.* What a revolutionary thing to say.

Maybe I'm wrong. He is the greatest guy, so I'm going to run up and just give him a big hug and tell him how happy I am to see him. I'm going to just go overcome how I feel.

And I did that and he went, *Hi, I'm so glad to see you!* And it was like magic. It was like magic. I spent a lot of time talking to him during that thing, learning about who he was. Of course we had never talked before, because I was being rude to him and he was reacting to it. You can see right there how we're changing a slide and seeing an entirely different uncle up there. Only he was always that way. I was malfunctioning and was seeing very unpleasant things that I created. I just put it together, and it appeared up there.

This is what we're going to accomplish. As we stop bringing out the worst in people and start bringing out the best in people, guess what the world starts looking like? You start going through your day wondering where all these nice people came from.

Where have they been? *I had the most pleasant exchange picking up my dry cleaning. It was just amazing. And over at McDonald's, they smiled at me! I don't know what everybody's on these days, but it's quite pleasant out there.* We had no idea that we were in charge of the world we lived in that what we were manufacturing in our projection booth is what we actually got out there.

You can see how valuable it's going to be to really look at this. This isn't being done to go make some other people feel better; they might not feel better when we make amends. It's being done so we can get rid of the broken, incorrect slides and create a different future for ourselves.

Maybe it's going to make some people feel better. Maybe it's going to have positive results when we actually go do the ninth step. The eighth step strictly has to do with readjusting things in the projection booth for ourselves. Bill suggests a few slides that you might have in your collection of how to get along with people.

I copied them down out of the book. How about anger? *I just like to go around with sort of a grimace so that people don't screw with me.* If you give them that look, they just leave you alone—you don't have to worry about it. I'm really scared to death.

You go, *Really? What kind of results do you get?*

People don't like me that much. I don't have that many close friends, but at least nobody's taking advantage of me, I can tell you that. That may be your slide.

What else do we have? How about lying?
Where were you?
Playing golf.
Then your buddy comes home and says, *Wasn't that movie great?*
I thought you said you were playing golf?
I was just kidding.
Then we wonder why nobody trusts us.
What's the matter?
They always ask where I'm going. She doesn't trust me.
Well, do you wonder why?

Tom I. has fifty years in AA, and I was talking to him at a convention one time, and I said, *Tom, do you have a problem with lying?*

He said, *It's the first thing out of my mouth. Somewhere when I was little, I learned that the truth could be dangerous. If I'm over here and somebody asks where I was, I say, "On the farm. No, actually I was over here."* He always corrects himself but he still finds this pattern.

I was sharing with him that I remember doing that exact same thing. I've been sober a long time and I finally get to retire a little bit up in Washington. I went out and dragged my little golf cart around every day trying to break 80. You golfers know. Finally one day, I had a 78, and there was the scorecard to prove it. I could hardly wait to see my AA golfing buddies.

I said, *I got news! I got news! Sit down. I want to tell you guys something! I had a 77!* A 78 was a wonderful thing, and then I had to go back later and go, *You know I was lying. I really had a 78.*

They said, *Well, we don't believe that, either.* I ruined the whole thing when the truth was absolutely acceptable and wonderful. I had to change it. You could see that changed a little bit how we got along.

Unfaithfulness is devastating, and we just say, *I don't know. I can't believe how that happened.* There's something that needs to get changed.

It's more prevalent. In the Big Book, when Bill is talking about the various problems, like owing money, he mentions being unfaithful to our wives and being way behind on the alimony. That's a common problem!

Miserly? *I got the money but I'm not going to dole it out. I'm just going to make them suffer. I know that they think I could help them.* You might do that with your kids. *Yeah, I'm sorry, the budget's too tight. I got to say no to you.*

Callous, very indifferent? *I just graduated from college! Good deal. Big deal. I'm glad you did, man.*

Each one of us has some of these slides, and this is our way of interacting. Who knows how we got started on it? It may go way back, but this becomes our little deal. Somebody gets promoted at work and we go, *Why didn't I get promoted?* We barely congratulate him. *Nice going.* We don't want to really add to their joy but to subtract from their joy.

Why? Why not participate in their happiness? *I don't know, I'm sort of a joy killer.*

Cynical, what a weapon that is.

Yeah, I just decided to go to college, Dad. I'm going to work my way through.

Well we'll see.

That really gave him a lot of confidence, didn't it? *Yeah, we'll see.* Almost like, *I seriously doubt it.* We play that one.

Cold. That look—not involved, just like ice. Why do we do that? We can protect our emotions. We're never going to get involved, we'll never get hurt—just stay Mr. Loner.

Impatient. *OK, how long is this going to take?* You ever do that? You just drive people crazy when they're trying to get stuff done?

Critical. I think everybody in the room knows how that works. *Yeah, it's nice, but are you sure you like this color? I know you painted it and you think it's a good color, but have you asked anybody else about the color that you chose for your house? Are you sure you asked people about those drapes? I don't want to say that it's not perfect, but…* Why is that?

Dominating. We can feel safe because we're in charge, and we just dominate. Sometimes with new members, I'll go, *Listen, we're going out to dinner tonight. I want you to listen to the amount of time that each person talks.*

We're there for thirty minutes, and that person talked twenty-eight. There was no room for anybody else to participate, and he didn't even realize it. Dominating. *I like me the most, and I'm sure everybody else would like to hear about me the most! It's the most exciting thing there is! Let me tell you one more story about me, and then you'll see how wonderful it is.*

Gossip. What's there to say? We want to get rid of it, but it's too much fun. As I said earlier, we give up originating it, and we simply become a telephone wire to allow it to go from this side of the room to that, where it's supposed to be going anyway—*I'm just helping. I'm really not a gossiper. I'm simply passing on information that may be useful to this side of the room about your misfortune.*

My favorite, which is very prevalent in AA, is self-pity. That's the first time I ever saw a sentence where it said we inflict self-pity on others. You know what that is? It's just never smiling.

Hey we're going to go to the baseball game.

I don't feel that it would be fun; I don't know why I should go. Let me tell you what happened to me. Matter of fact, I'll tell you what happened to me at the game. Because I don't want you to enjoy the game at all. I just want to tell you what he said or what he did. It's the seventh inning now, and I'm still going on and on and on about my problems.

We're going to start changing our repertoire of behavior. We've collected these; this is what we put in the projector. *That situation*—click—*covered.* We're going to see what it causes and what it causes us to see, and then we're going to come up with a new plan, which is to live in harmony.

How can I adjust to them instead of making them adjust to me? That is a totally different guaranteed winning perspective. I'll give you an example of that—it was discussed up in Maine at one of the meetings.

The discussion was, *Groups are stopping the Lord's Prayer at meetings and switching to the Serenity Prayer. What do we think about that?* Every group's autonomous; they can do any damn thing they want. So it came down to motives. If in a group, somebody said, *Wouldn't it be fun to learn a Jewish prayer and sing it at our meeting to welcome our Jewish friends?*, and everybody liked it, that would be a very spiritual and wonderful change. On the other hand, if the reason for changing was, *I don't like it. It offends me*, what principle are we putting in there? We're trying to learn spirituality, not politics. Spirituality. The principle of the program is to teach us to adjust to the situation and not demand that the situation adjust to us.

That would be a lousy reason for changing from a spiritual point of view. You see the difference? The difference is night and day. *I want this changed because it bothers me.* That's self-pity, self-centered. Once we get over that and can be happy with whatever the group decision is, we're going to see a whole different world up there, not one that has to be changed to fit my self-centeredness. Anyway, we get to the end of the line: "Amends themselves are the cleansing agent in all these slides." That is what erases them. The willingness to make these amends and then to go out and to actually contact the people (with letters or in person or by phone or whatever our sponsor advises) takes all of this past pattern and gets rid of it.

We are going to start seeing a totally different world. The step really is something that's going to benefit us all. From a spiritual point of view, this is where we really start making huge spiritual changes and breakthroughs, so much so that the promises come after the next step.

Those promises are the biggest deal in AA. Look where they're coming. They're coming right here when we're going to go in and fix the interpersonal relationship slides. What could we say? Be thorough. Think of everything where you were obnoxious. Don't leave anything out, because you are going to be the beneficiary as you watch all of this disappear and this new world appear in its place.

9

The Spiritual Life is Not a Theory

NOT TOO MUCH happened in the '70s. In 1970, they had the International Convention in Miami, which was the thirty-fifth anniversary of Alcoholics Anonymous, and the theme was Unity. Bill Wilson gave his last talk. He was quite ill with emphysema, and he was scheduled to speak, but the word was around that he would not be able to make it. My friend Clancy was there, and he was talking to another old-timer, older than Clancy, and Clancy said, *Well, it looks like he is just too weak to talk.* The other guy said, *He will talk. Guarantee you—he will talk.*

I'll be darned—at the last minute, the ambulance pulls up. Bill gets out and gives his talk. As they took him offstage after, Clancy said, *Well, how did you know?*

He said, *Well, in 1950, Dr. Bob got out of his deathbed and gave his last talk at the convention in Cleveland. I knew Bill wanted to give his last talk.* Shortly thereafter, on January 24, 1971, Bill passed away. We owe a great deal to Dr. Bob and to Bill, and I just am such an admirer of Bill. One of my greatest regrets is that my friends in Washington would go up to the Bill Wilson Dinner every year, and I wouldn't. They'd ask me to go, and I'd say, *I don't have enough money.* It probably would have cost $70 or something like that to go up.

I remember my friend Hal saying, *You know, he is not going to last forever. You are going to really regret that you never met him.*

Ask me if I regret it? That would have been such an honor, but it didn't happen.

In 1972, Nell Wing started our archives in the General Service Office. They have newspaper stories from all the way back to the first time AA was mentioned in the newspapers. Oddly enough, on the same page was a story about somebody over in Germany that was rising up and was going to save the country and I often thought about, *There it is, on the front page of New York Times—this thing called AA and this thing called Hitler.* Talk about good and evil appearing all at once, and the amount of good that has been done by AA is just immeasurable.

The next year, "Came to Believe" was published, and sales of our Big Book reached one million copies. They had a ceremony in the White House and gave it to President Nixon, who probably should have read it. (Just observing. I am not taking his inventory.)

Then in '75, "Living Sober" was published; that's the second biggest seller after the Big Book. It's really popular amongst AA members. In 1976, the third edition came out, and in 1978 sales reached two million Big Books. It only took four years to go from 1 million to 2 million, after taking all those years to get there. Then in 1979, Ernest Kurtz came out with his wonderful history book, "Not God," where he did a Ph.D. dissertation on our fellowship. It is one of the better analyses of the dynamics of our history, and it's well worth reading when you get interested in history. [*A revised edition is now published with the title "AA: The Story" –Ed.*]

Now there was another story that I want to talk about and then I'll get to the ninth step. When I was in the Marine Corps many years ago, I was on a presentation team that traveled around the country and even the world giving an overview of the Marine Corps and how it would be in the future. They had a hypothetical situation. Oddly enough, way back then, it was set in the middle east. It was headed by a General, Chet Huntley, and David Brinkley introduced it, and then we went through and showed all of the weapons, the fighter planes, the tanks, the artillery, the communications, and the supply. The whole thing had slides and movies—it took about eight hours to show the enormity of the operation.

At the end of the show, the General would come out and he would say, "Ladies and gentlemen, all of the things you have seen, all of this only serves one purpose." And then it flashed a slide of a Marine infantry E1 or E2 with a rifle, and he would say, "To make his job easier." That's the whole point. Everything was to make his job easier, because that's where the rubber meets the road—that's where everything gets done. The reason I tell that is to make an analogy to Alcoholics Anonymous. We have the General Service Office, the General Service Conference, international activities, publications and pamphlets, intergroup offices and 200,000 groups in over a hundred countries. We have this enormous mothership known as AA. And when you think about it, all of that is just there to facilitate and enable one alcoholic talking to another alcoholic. That's where it happens. That is why AA works. All the rest of it just supports that. Our clubs, our dances—all of that just supports that.

It is absolutely essential to understand the process of identification, because identification is how a new alcoholic connects to AA in a way that glues them in with sufficient bonding effect so that they are safe from alcohol. When you think about it, if you are going to go see a therapist about your alcoholism, you go in the office and the therapist says, *Well, tell me all about you.* But when AAs are going on a Twelve-Step call to a new person, they say, *Let us tell you all about us.* It's exactly the opposite, and we just sit there and tell our entire story. Sometimes we bring two people, and two people will tell their entire story.

When I got sober, we went to just speaker meetings for at least three months before we went to a discussion meeting, so that we would hear stories and identify. The old saying was, *Somebody told my story. They stood up there and said they hid the vodka in the toilet and they did this and they … my God! That's exactly the same!* I felt this 100 percent connection with the fellowship of Alcoholics

Anonymous and with the person that was going to help me. As a sponsor, I also make the same bonding with the new alcoholic.

I can remember the first time I went on a Twelve-Step call for a periodic, and he told me that sometimes he stayed sober for two months before he drank again.

I thought, *I don't know anything about that. I don't know what he is talking about.*

I went back to my sponsor and he said, *Well, we got a couple of periodics in the group. So we are going to get their help. They are going to go with you the next time and then there will be a connection made.*

I had this feeling that I was the wrong person to talk to a periodic, because we weren't exactly the same. It's that exact sameness that creates the bond that keeps us sober when Dr. Alcohol comes knocking on the door. That's a very important thing. Back then, fifty percent of the people who came to AA never drank again, twenty-five percent would slip around little bit and then they would never drink again, and of the other twenty-five percent, some of those made it.

I think I had four months before I heard about a slip. I said, *What's that?*

Somebody out from Manassas asked, *What is that?*

My sponsor said, *You're not allowed to have one.* I got faked into thinking that there were classes of people: those allowed to have one and those that weren't. Any time I thought about having a drink, I went, *Oh, I'm not allowed. Gee whiz.* I got sober with two other guys; we called ourselves the Class of '64. I am the only one left, but all three of us never took a drink.

Back then, everyone was dual addicted. All of the meetings were smoking meetings. All of them. Smoking sent up a craving that you could hardly get through the meeting. I mean it just was such a thing. You had to get money; you had to steal cigarettes if you didn't have one. We knew it was killing us. It killed a whole bunch of AAs—still does. It killed Bill Wilson. It's a fatal addiction, but no one tried to use AA to stop smoking. We didn't identify ourselves as alcoholics and nicotine addicts; we didn't say an alcoholic nonsmoker couldn't sponsor an alcoholic smoker, so that they would feel different from one another. It wasn't brought into the equation. We used AA principles to stop smoking, but outside of AA. In other words, everything was kept *just alcohol.*

Now, I use the analogy of our space shuttle, which is kind of like the big mothership of Alcoholics Anonymous. The thing that's been making the headlines over the past few years is that the tiles are coming off; those tiles are put on there to protect it from temperatures from -1,000 up to +3,000, mostly during re-entry, when the stress is the greatest. There is great consternation when that happens, because if enough of them come off, they could endanger the whole ship. When it happened, they went the manufacturer and they really raised hell. They said, *They weren't put on right. The bonding was not adequate to withstand the turmoil of the re-entry.*

The manufacturer had to go along with that. He couldn't say, *No, it wasn't that. The earth's atmosphere has changed, and there is more friction in the atmosphere now, and that's what's causing them to go off.* No, it is that the bonding wasn't tight enough. We hear a lot about how, in today's world, addiction is different than it used to be, and that's why the percentage of people recovering is dropping. We take that into account. We just go, *Well, it must be something else, but I will submit to you that it is the bonding to this program that is going to protect each one of us during re-entry when the rubber meets the road. Am I going to be held tight enough to not go flying off into alcoholism's space out there?*

If you want to find what has been written about it, I would suggest something that Bill Wilson wrote, "Problems Other Than Alcohol." I mean, back then they had pill addicts, a lot of drug problems … and so he thought carefully about what AA should do about all these things, and he wrote this pamphlet. As you know, the decision was made to make AA itself exclusive and to give authorization to anybody with a different type of problem permission to use AA's Twelve Steps, and we have a hundred other problems—over a hundred—that are using the Twelve Steps of Alcoholics Anonymous. There is absolutely no problem if five or six alcoholic drug addicts want to form a group of alcoholic drug addicts; it just wouldn't be an AA meeting. It would be the same steps, it would be the same everything, but when they met, they would be bonding perfectly.

I will give you one final analogy. When you have a magnifying glass, you can use it to read small print, but you can also use it to start a fire. You can use the power of the sun to actually cause small twigs and leaves to ignite and start a fire. I am going to call that fire a spiritual awakening. Now, that's done by taking the magnifying glass and bringing the circle of light down to a pinpoint, and then—*boom*. It would be possible to move the magnifying glass in a little bit and have a spot about an inch in diameter, which would make the ground right there much warmer than it was. It would be kind of warm and fuzzy, and it would be more inclusive. You could include more of the ground getting warm and we can do the same thing. We can open doors wider and wider and have a bigger segment of the population feel wonderfully warm, welcome, and fuzzy—hugs and dances and all of the wonderful things. But when re-entry takes place, warm and fuzzy won't cut it. It's just not going to work.

I just want to make a pitch for this particular topic. I imagine an AA dance, and I imagine people having the most wonderful time. For the purposes of my story, I have a lady named Mary, who has eight months sober. She has never felt happier in her life. Being in this fellowship has made her appreciate life like she has never appreciated it before, and she has new friends and a new purpose and feels just wonderful about herself. No intention of drinking. She is just at the dance, and a black car pulls up like the Batmobile. A guy gets out, and we are nervous already as he gets out of the car. He's kind of tall, dark, mysterious, with a cape. He comes into the dance, and you could see everybody at the dance go, *Ooh, who is that?* He looks at his dance card and goes right over to Mary, taps her on the shoulder and she turns around. He says, *Hi! My name is John Barleycorn. May I cut in?*

There is a kind of a warning feeling in her gut, but she says, *Sure.* They dance a couple of dances and he says, *Why don't we get out of here and go really have some fun?* She drives off in his car and maybe six months later, even six years later, the car pulls back up, and she is dropped on the road, half-dead.

There wasn't any protection when the disease knocked, and the difference is realized when the bonding is complete and we have been led to an awakening. The same situation happens and the same car pulls up and the same Barleycorn comes over with a dance card with Mary's name on it. He taps her on the shoulder. She turns around, and John Barleycorn sees God standing there and says, *Oh, never mind*, and leaves. She is completely unaware that there was ever any danger or what could have possibly happened. She was dancing in a position of neutrality. Dancing in a position of neutrality. That car could pull up fifty times a night, and she would just stay there dancing having a wonderful time.

I just offer it up to think about, because I'm old. AA has done well for seventy-two years and has done well by me for forty-two years, but you guys are going to be around a lot longer than that. I am just asking you to think about this mothership and how tight the tiles are. I was up in Maine a couple of weeks ago and I gave a modified version of this little pitch, and afterwards there were several irate people who came up to read me the riot act. One of them was a young lady who said I had ruined her life. She said, *I joined OA (Overeaters Anonymous) some time ago, and it didn't work at all. So I went to AA. I went to an AA group and asked them to have a group conscience requesting that I could become a full-fledged member. They agreed, and now I can sponsor alcoholics.*

I said, *Well, we're really not discussing the fifth tradition here— primary purpose. We are now discussing the fourth tradition—each group is autonomous, and that means that any AA group can do something really stupid. It's just like the Richmond group did when they served booze at meetings. It just didn't last very long and it didn't work.*

I was recently working with a new guy, and we spent a lot of time on the first step and identification until I felt that I absolutely was connected with him and he was connected with me.

And then I said, *OK, now we are ready to go through the rest of the steps for the spiritual awakening.*

He said, *You really think it will happen?*

I said, *Well, let me put it this way. I'm as sure that it will happen as I am when I put water in the freezer that it will turn into ice. I can't guarantee it, but I'm pretty damn sure that it is going to turn into ice.*

It is your mothership, and you are going to be the ones 30 years from now. Maybe the whole fellowship will be going through a turmoil. I don't know. Some kind of inter-disputes or getting into trouble. The *Washington Post* just had a big story about an AA group in Washington that really did some bad stuff. As the mothership goes through some kind of a major challenge, will the individual tiles stay on? That's all I am asking. Will they stay on? Will they be bonded tight enough?

Now we move on to the ninth step and start the amends process, and it is a very powerful eraser of the past events. Admitting you are wrong is one of the hardest things for the human ego to do, not knowing what's going to happen, and dealing with things that we have been carrying around. They wouldn't be on our list if we weren't carrying them around. This list of harm we did others doesn't come from letters. It's not from people requesting, *Add me to the list.* We are already carrying it. We carry it around day and night—the harm we have done others—because there is a part of us that doesn't want to harm people, and that's the part we want to get to know. How do we know what's going to happen when we go make these amends?

That's when Bill writes the spiritual life is not a theory. We have to live it, and this is a huge risk. I remember that story about the man who had robbed ten homes. He told his sponsor he didn't want to go there, and he said, *Let's try staying sober without going there*. A few years went by, and finally he said, *I can't take it anymore. I've got to go see all those people whose homes I broke into.* And he did. The sponsor went with him. They went at six o'clock at night. He pulled up, and he coached him to say, *I am the man who broke into your house five years ago and took a whole bunch of your stuff. I will be glad to wait here if you want to call the cops, but I am in AA. I am a sober alcoholic now, and I am trying to make amends.* Now, those people could have called the cops. He could have gone right to jail, but he had to do that in order to stay sober, because his mind would not allow him the peace until he had done it. But each one of them did not call the cops.

Some of them just said, I am so glad you came back to tell me who it was that I am going to just let it go. Other people said, *Well, I would like some financial reimbursement—$500*, and he would say, *Well, I can pay $25 a week.* He made all the settlements till he got to the last house; a lady answered the door, and he told her what the situation was. Then he said, *I would like to make amends*, and she said, *You already did.* He didn't understand what she was saying, so she got her husband.

She said, *Tell my husband what you just told me.* So he told him, and they both said the same thing: *Oh my God, you have really made amends to us. Until you came up tonight, we always believed that our son did it and was lying. Now we know that we were wrong.* The family was reunited through that process.

In my own life I had a story like that. Now I'd been sober about twenty-five years. You know the memory bubbles will sometimes come popping up and then you've got one more amend to make. I was getting ready to watch the Redskins play up in Washington, which was a big deal—like watching the Bucs down here in Tampa. I'd gotten everything done. I was in my little townhouse and I had Coca-Colas, potato chips and the whole deal. It was about ten minutes till game time, and here comes this memory bubble.

Hey, you remember Bill Marcie? You went through flight school with him. You'd always be broke, and you'd have to borrow the rent money from him until payday.

Yeah, yeah, good drinking buddy.

Well, you remember the time that you didn't pay him?

Not until now, but I do. Yeah I remember. He got transferred ahead of me to the next duty station, and I said, "I'll catch you when we…" Then when I got there it never came up, and on and on.

So it was $70. I said, *Where am I going to find Bill Marcie? I don't know where he is. I haven't got a clue.*

Well, why don't you look?

I'm not going to look. The Redskins game is coming on. I'm having this conflict with my own conscience, and it won't let up.

I said, *It's Sunday. I can't call the Marine Corps and find out.*

Well, think about it. What did he do?

Well, he liked to ski.

OK, well, then try some place where they ski.

Well, where do they ski?

I don't know.

Colorado, I think they ski in Vermont.

Well, try Vermont.

All right, I'll try it. It was really getting annoying. I said, *I'm going to try Vermont, and that's it. If he's not there, screw it. I'll do it later.* So I called information. He had a long name: William P. Marcie, III. I called information in Vermont and asked if they possibly had a listing for him. I waited impatiently … there is!

All right, what's the number? What's the number? Now I'm dialing the number because it's just like three minutes to kick off. I said, *He won't be in. What are the odds on him being in? He won't be in, but at least I dialed the number.*

Hello?

Hello, Bill. Hey, it's Sandy Beach—do you remember me?

Oh yes, Sandy, how are you?

Oh geez, well, listen, Bill—I got to get right to the point here. I joined AA a long time ago, and it's really wonderful. It's just the

greatest thing in the world, but we make amends, and I just had this
memory bubble of the $70 that I owed you.

Then he said, *I really vaguely remember it—just forget it.*

No, I can't forget it Bill. I got to send it up there. What's your
address?

So, he gave me the address up in Vermont, and he was running
a gift shop at a ski resort. So, anyway, I just told him how happy
I was and how well things are going. Then I said, *I got to go, Bill.*
I'll call you some other time, and I hung up. Then a few days later,
I added like $250 for interest and mailed it off. About two weeks
after that, I got a box from the gift shop of probably $400 worth
of stuff that he sent down. Then, he called me once and told me he
was moving to North Carolina and we had to get together. I had
the phone number, and then it just went out the window.

And about eight years later, I was speaking in North Carolina.
At the end of the talk, this lady came up and said, *I'd like to intro-*
duce myself—my name is Kathy Marcie. It's such an unusual name.

I said, *Oh, Bill Marcie's wife?*

She said, *No, his widow.*

I said, *Oh, I'm so sorry.* Then, I looked at her and I said, *What*
are you doing here? She said, *I'm an Al-Anon. After you called him*
and told him how wonderful AA was and what it has done for you,
he joined, and he had five years when he died. So, all amends are
part of a bigger picture that we haven't got a clue about, and they
will be revealed as we get the courage to go out and do this very
thoroughly. After discussing it with our sponsor to determine the
most harmonious way to do the amends and going through with it,
something unbelievable happens to those slides and the world that
we live in.

I wrote down some of the wonderful changes. Some of you may
have heard about them already. We're going to look up there and
see "a new freedom and a new happiness" that wasn't there before.
We've never even seen it before. All we were doing was knocking
on doors, making amends. We're going to look up and "not regret

the past" and see that the past has no power over us. It's been completely lifted. How many of us carried burdens from the past? And now, we have no regrets about it. It's an open book. That wasn't up there before. There's a whole new reality that is being revealed as the result of following these steps. We look up and for the first time see "serenity and we will know peace," just from calling somebody up and saying *I'm sorry*. Well, that's what God asked us to do, and this is what He decided to give us as a result of that. "That feeling of uselessness and self-pity will disappear." How about that? Self-pity will disappear. Can you see the paint removers coming over the slide of self-pity, and it just turns into liquid. It just washes off there. It just isn't there. "Self-seeking will slip away." That's even more amazing. It doesn't get figured out.

We don't suddenly learn how to be not selfish. It just deserts us. It just goes out the back. That's the amazing part of this. We're not directly trying to have any of this happen. We're just doing these stupid things that our sponsor asks us to do. That's all we're doing. The booth is getting cleaned out and is being transformed. "Our whole attitude and outlook on life will change." Do you know how big that is? Everything that you used to see when you got up and walked out the door is gone, and there is a whole new thing to see when you walk out there. That's remarkable.

This is not small stuff. "Fear of people and of economic insecurity will leave us," fear of losing money disappears. We suddenly realize that we're getting answers from a different place, from our intuitions and they can only be activated when we let go. Every time, that's why we let go. *Oh, I got this thing I'm agonizing over.* Stop agonizing. Let it go. Go to the movies. Write a poem. Go sit down and write an eight-line poem about flying, and allow God to contact you through your intuitions.

This happens all the time. It occurs to you—*here's the answer.* That's our highest level. That's where we operate when we're not disturbed. Then the jackpot is we suddenly realize God's doing this. Now, up until then, God was something we knew about. We had read about Him. We had gone to a church and we knew all about Him. We knew about all the miracles. We knew this, we knew that, and we knew more about Him than anybody else in the Sunday school class.

But we never had contact until now. When it says, "we will suddenly realize," that's what we see. The light of our Higher Power shines through us and produces a new world, and we're aware of it. So we get back to the beginning of the Big Book where it says, "The absolute certainty that our Creator has entered our hearts and lives in a way which is indeed miraculous." If that hasn't happened to you yet, you're missing out on the whole point of the program. It's all in the steps, with a guide, with proper bonding and identification to go and experience. This is the jackpot. This is the awakening. Then we try to maintain it and expand it and share it.

We've gone in and changed the slides. It's been around for a lot of years, transforming what's inside of us—and we transform the world. The one you live in. That's all any human being can ever do, to transform the world that they live in from a very painful, uncomfortable Goddamn world into one where you can see and understand why you're alive, what the whole deal is. Life makes sense, and we become a very small minority in the population of planet Earth that understands the world in this light.

This is something that people would love, only they don't know it's missing. They think they need a new TV. They're going to work on changing that screen until they die. We, the alcoholics, forced into this damned program called AA—we really were the chosen few.

Somehow, whatever it is, I am going to take that rotten crowd, and I am going to single them out for something special, provided they pass it on to the next person. We really have a noble calling here. It is not just, *Oh, I am going to hang around and go to a meeting.* This is really a big deal. It's really fun, and I hope you all see the picture of how much fun it can be.

10

No Editorial Desired
or Required

WE ARE UP to the '80s. We started in the '30s and the very origins of Alcoholics Anonymous—even before the '30s, when the Oxford Movement was getting started—and we sort of tracked through all of the decades and we come to 1980.

1980 was a big deal for me. In the beginning of that year, some people that I knew invited me up to New Jersey, and they said, *We're having a little roundup here, and we want you to come up and speak at it.* I went up there, and I could tell there was a lot of tension in the room. Everybody was dressed up. I couldn't quite put my finger on it, but Lois Wilson was there, and I got to meet her. The guy said to me, *Now really do good!*, which is the perfect thing to tell somebody when you don't know what's going on.

I just did my stuff, and then they said, *We'll let you know. Just wait here.* Let me know? Do I get the collection? It turned out that it was an audition to see if I was going to speak in the Superdome at AA's anniversary over in New Orleans, and I passed. I'm glad I didn't know it ahead of time, or that would have been a disaster. In 1980, AA's forty-fifth anniversary was held in New Orleans, which is really a wonderful city for a bunch of people who don't drink. I still can remember—this happens at all the Internationals—the vendors were no slouches and they had done their homework. They were selling Bill Wilson hotdogs on the corner, and they had signs outside the bars that they had these wonderful non-alcoholic drinks—things with fruit and little umbrellas, called the Serenity Sling or the Turning Point. They had ginger ale and this and that—and they were $3, so they were making money off of the drunks. They had 23,000 people there, and that Friday night was kind of a disaster.

They had the flag ceremony on that night, and they had told the countries that when they brought their flag up, they could say one or two words, like, "The great state of Alabama, home of the blah, blah, blah!" We're talking about grinding out an hour and a half or something on that, and we're sitting on the stage waiting to talk and desperately needing to go to the bathroom, and this went on. Then there was a miscommunication. They always have the local congressman or congresswoman give a welcome, and her staff assistant was in AA. Somehow the word got out that she was to give her full speech, which was thirty minutes; that was Lindy Boggs, who was from a great New Orleans family. Her daughter is Cokie Roberts—you watch her on the Sunday News. Anyway, she talked for thirty minutes, and then they started with the celebrities, and then they started with a lot of other things, and I was last. They had three speakers of twenty minutes each, and I could see the people leaving. I mean, they were just tired. They just were going home. I would guess that probably 7,000 or 8,000 people had gone before it was my turn, but it was a big honor.

That same year, Marty Mann passed away. Of course, Marty Mann was one of the first women to get sober in AA and became very interested in education about alcoholism and started the National Council, which became the National Institute on Alcohol and Alcohol Abuse. She started all of the efforts to make alcoholism a disease, so it could be covered by insurance, which led to the treatment centers.

It became something that was entirely different than it used to be when the only way people got to AA was through word of mouth: *Yeah, my uncle is in there. I'll get you in touch with him.* Now we have employers and judges and all kinds of people that funnel new alcoholics into AA.

In '81, the Big Book hit 3 million. It's just staggering to watch the numbers as they take off. It took all those years to get to 1 million and three years to get to 3 million. In '82, the estimated membership was just under 1 million, and we had 48,000 groups in the world. You can see how it went from three groups and 35 members up to 48,000 groups all around the world.

Nell Wing retired. She was the archivist and was Bill Wilson's secretary, and she typed the Twelve and Twelve. She started the archives in New York, and then a guy named Frank Mouser took over, whom I became very good friends with. I just loved going up there. Frank would come to conventions, and he had a big presentation with slides about the history of AA. He really knew lots of obscure things that were of interest to me and other weird people. He retired over on the East Coast of Florida, and I had all these plans to get him over here to talk at different groups. But he died of a heart attack, I think less than a year after he retired, and it was one of the great losses of resources that we have had.

OK, in '85 we had the big one, the fiftieth anniversary of Alcoholics Anonymous up in Montreal, Canada. We went up to 44,000 people at that convention. AA was starting to become one of the largest conventions held in the world.

At that convention, the gal that typed the Big Book spoke—Ruth Hock. Now, that is really going back to the very beginning. They gave her the five millionth copy of the Big Book, and the celebration was quite wonderful. A very obscure fact (but a true one) is that the Seagram's Distillery, which is right there in Montreal—maker of lots of whiskey that I consumed, such as Seagram's 7 which was very affordable—had their three flags at half-mast. The Canadian flag, the British flag and the Seagram's family crest were all at half-mast for the entire time that Alcoholics Anonymous was in town. They got some good publicity out of it.

Later in that year, to show that there are some screw-ups that can happen, it was discovered that the copyright on the first edition and the second edition had somehow been let to expire. That opened the door for other publishers to print copies of the Big Book. It turns out, it really hasn't affected our literature sales that much. There was this great fear that one of AA's big sources of income was going to be seriously affected, but it really wasn't. All the intergroups kept buying their books from New York. If you ever ended up with a copy that was done by some other publishing company, that's the reason. It's interesting to know that Hazelden did not take advantage of that. Hazelden has really been a friend of AA, and they sell more literature and buy more Big Books than almost anyone. They just are of tremendous assistance to Alcoholics Anonymous. Also, Bill and Lois's home in Bedford, New York, Stepping Stones, was declared a New York Historical Site. It's been preserved, and it's there for us to visit.

AA membership reached one million, so that's astounding alone—a million people have gotten sober on a message. A message has been passed from one person to another—that's what happened. A million people heard it and had their lives transformed, because that's how it works. It's just one of us talking to another one.

We have a support system, but the real action takes place in the individual groups when somebody new arrives. *Anybody want to get a white chip?* You remember that, and up you come and then people come around you, and pretty soon you're getting a ninety-day chip. Then you're getting a year chip, and then you're handing out a white chip to somebody, and it's just nice—a million people. In 1986, the paperback edition came out of the Big Book, and a lot of people liked that it was lighter and you could carry it around. I have one of each (The Twelve and Twelve paperback edition came out in 1989).

In '87, we were getting a lot of different ideas in AA. *Well, I think we ought to do this, I think we ought to do that.* There was just a lot of pressure to go in a million different directions, and so the

General Service Conference met.

They made it very clear that our preamble was not going to be changed. *Well, we ought to have it redone, we ought to include this, we ought to get this, we ought to do that.* It was absolutely unanimous from all over—*The preamble is going to stay the way it is. And besides that, we're going to print up cards, send them out to all the groups, about our primary purpose, what a closed meeting and what an open meeting is, just to clarify all of that.* AA just made a decision: Stick to the basics, do what we do best. It was formally adopted in '87.

In '88, Lois Wilson died at 97 years of age. Now, that is astounding that she was there from '35 to '88 and saw all this happen, and Al-Anon blossomed into the wonderful fellowship that it is. We're seeing now just about everybody from way back then isn't around anymore.

Bill passed the torch way back when he stepped down and allowed the fellowship to govern itself and to take care of itself, and it's been doing that ever since. We'll never have two co-founders again. There'll never be anybody who wrote all our literature or anything like that.

It's interesting to look back at that literature; a lot of the language is kind of archaic today. We don't use the same adjectives, we don't use the same type of sentences, but people of seventeen years of age connect with it. *Yeah, I was reading the book. It really helped me.* There's a message in there that's amazing.

That year, "The Language of the Heart" was published. If there was anything that describes AA, it's "The Language of the Heart." It's one heart speaking to another—it's not intellect. People give talks, and they speak from their heart, and you connect and you realize you're in the right place that nobody is here with an angle. They just want to help you, and then once we make it, then we help each other stay here, and this continues to grow.

Leonard Strong was Bill's brother-in-law. He was a doctor and he died in '89. He really was of tremendous assistance. He paid for Bill to go to treatment. He was the one that got him the appointment with Willy Richardson in Rockefeller's office. A lot of wonderful things happened as a result of the advisory board in the Rockefeller Foundation. He himself was on the board in the very beginning of our alcoholic foundation. He really was someone who took an interest in Bill and then in AA and carried it on till when he died in 1989. That year, James Woods and James Garner played Bill Wilson and Dr. Bob in a big Hallmark movie, "My Name Is Bill W."

People watched that and really learned about AA. The producers had consulted with New York on that film, and so when you see it, it really is real. *Yeah, that's just like my group!* It gave us more credibility and helped people get over the stigma of alcoholism, which is very small now.

You rarely hear somebody say, *Gee, they found out I'm an alcoholic at work, and they're letting me go.* (A sober alcoholic. They ought to let us go if we're a drunk alcoholic.)

We come to the tenth step, and if we were to rewrite it to fit our ongoing analogy, it would say, "Continued to only inventory the projection booth and, when we found something wrong, promptly admitted it." Why are we inventorying? This is the master switch from inventorying the big screen to only inventorying ourselves as a way of straightening out the world.

Instead of imagining ourselves as human beings who are living in a messy world that we're trying to straighten out, we imagined that there were all these terrible things going on and we were being treated unfairly. We were up there on the screen trying to change them. *I'll move this guy over here and I ought to move that guy over there.* The reason it's screwed up is what you're projecting from the projection booth—you are putting that story up there. If you go inside through our process of our steps and inventory all your old ideas with your sponsor and start transforming what's being shown up there, you're going to find what we call an awakening.

You're going to find that when you look at the world, it's a much happier and better place than you ever dreamed. We found that the process really was of getting rid of things. Spirituality is not done by getting anything or learning anything. Knowledge is not part of it. Getting rid of knowledge *is* part of it—getting rid of ideas until there's nothing left except being you, with no judgments on it. We simply exist every day and we don't editorialize on the events that are happening. They just are. The editorializing was our problem, and it's been every human being's problem since God knows when. It isn't what happens in life, it's how we describe it to ourselves.

Imagine if somebody forgot to save you a hotdog. There were ten of us, and there were only nine hotdogs; you ended up not getting one. *All right, what's the deal? One guy didn't get a hotdog. OK, that's the headline: one guy didn't get a hotdog.* How is that filed away for that guy? What's his editorial on it? *The biggest insult in the world was done to me today by a group of insensitive people whom I will never speak to again.* There were only nine hotdogs—that had nothing to do with their respect for the tenth guy, but that's the story that got filed away.

We're producing all these slides, and when we look up there, we go, *No hotdog for me.* What we're seeing up there is driving us crazy, and we have no idea that we're doing it.

Now let me give you an example. About a month ago I was in my living room and I happened to be looking at the Big Book. I was just reading something out of the chapter "To the Agnostic." The lamp that I was using burned out. I went to the kitchen and I got another light bulb. I came back in and I took that lampshade off and I touched the bulb—it was OK with my handkerchief to unscrew it, but it was still a little hot.

I put the other bulb in, put the lampshade back on, went in the kitchen, threw the bulb away and continued reading. That's what I did. I didn't call my sponsor and ask him why a light would go out while I was reading the Big Book, sending me a signal that God doesn't like me and that I never should have been reading the Big Book in the first place. *I'm probably not sober, or that lamp never* would have gone out. *I can't believe that that would happen to me! I've never felt more rejected than I did when it went dark as I was reading the Big Book.* That's making quite a problem out of a bulb going out, isn't it? Don't we all do it? We just create this stuff and we are so good at it because we know how to press our own buttons better than anybody else does and we continuously do.

This is how the ego continues to exist and to dominate. As it continues, it creates a story that becomes our own reality. Once upon a time an actor got a job. He'd been looking for work for quite a while and he got a part in a Broadway show. The part he got actually had a very significant meaning in the play. He was a janitor. The play opened with the janitor on the first floor of a brokerage firm, sweeping the lobby. The lights come on, and people start coming to work, and then they're up in the offices on the second floor, where all the action is taking place. They're making the deals, running down, going by the janitor occasionally. As it turned out, when they had problems, they talked to him.

He really ends up being like the philosopher in the play, but he doesn't see it that way. He sees himself as a janitor sweeping the floor, which is what his part called for. For a month, he was so happy that he got the part because he was getting paid regularly. But the longer it went on, he started thinking, *Look at this. There are 500 people in this theater watching me sweep the freaking floor. They're looking at me going, "Hey, look at the janitor." I have a lot more talent than the guys upstairs, the brokers. I'm a much better actor than these other people in this show. This is really bordering on a tragedy of huge proportions. This is almost up at the "King Lear," the Shakespeare level. What is being done to a sensitive actor like me, placing me in a demeaning position in front of 500 people every night, is awful. It's a disgrace. This isn't a play about the stock brokerage firm! This is a play about a sensitive actor getting screwed.*

He carries this on to the point that that's the play he's in every night. He's in the play where he gets embarrassed and humiliated. We all are in our own play, and that's the one we're trying to break.

Those are the slides that are going up there; we've been putting them up there for years. We started out with the real play in childhood.

When we arrived here, we were in God's world. We hadn't made one comment about his world yet, but as soon as we began to be able to think about things, we started describing it to suit ourselves and ended up with a mess. Because we have the ability to think, the temptation to make ourselves the center of everything is overpowering. That's why we say self-centeredness is the problem. *Yes, this is the world as God created it, but he didn't make me important enough. I'm going to ratchet it up a little bit.* Each one of us has made ourselves the star of our own story. It's almost like a dream. We're the stars of our dreams; everything happens to us.

There was a tidal wave in Burma, and it ruined my day. I had to look at that. The tidal wave really happened to me. I wish it had happened later, because I was having a bad day, and that kind of pushed me over the edge. The tidal wave didn't happen to all the victims, it happened to me. This is what self-centeredness does, and this is why we go so wacky that we want relief from it and we drink. We get relief from that perspective. All we're doing as we become spiritual in this program is going back home, going back to what was there before we superimposed the story on top of it.

We get a glimpse of it as we're doing the first nine steps. We get that magic moment when we personally see through our own story and see a glimpse of God's kingdom when we feel financial insecurity leave us, when we feel self-seeking slipping away, when we suddenly realize that God is doing for us what we couldn't do for ourselves. We see it, and we start seeing the light from the projection booth that is inside of us, which is our spiritual light, now shining through some openings in the slides.

The more we can erase them and allow more light to come out, that light is what shines on the world as we go around, and the world is remarkably better than it ever was, because the light itself causes everyone to behave differently. And as we said in the last chapter, instead of bringing out the worst in people, we're bringing out the best. That transforms everyone that we run into into somebody nice. It's all because of us. We're generating the entire show all by ourselves. The Big Book really emphasizes this; it only has a couple of pages on the tenth step, but they are powerful. They are pure spirituality. If you want to read spiritual language, read several of the sentences in the Big Book. It's just amazing.

Here's a pretty big sentence: "We have entered the world of the spirit." We've gotten through nine steps and we've now entered the world of the spirit. What do you suppose that means? It means we got a glimpse of it, and we saw that our old way of doing things isn't that good. We've had a glimpse of something better, which has to do with abandoning old ideas. You decided life should be lived—remember all the rules we put together? *You have to get ahead in business. You have to screw this guy out of this. If you don't get your share, who's going to get it for you? Don't trust people; they're all bad. People are basically evil. Life makes no sense, so why even give a damn?* This is all stuff that's flying around, and those are your rules for living. *If somebody cuts me off once, I cut off three people. If somebody does this, I do that.*

Whatever they all were, we're going to abandon them. This is where we're just deciding to come into the world of the spirit. We're going to see what this consists of, and what this consists of is not paying any attention whatsoever to the screen. Stop paying any attention. That no longer is relevant.

What everybody else is doing is no longer relevant. Let's not even keep track of it. We're only going to focus on ourselves. I am going to get up every day and just look at myself and see what I can do to be spiritual. Bingo—right out of the block. Here's the problem with spirituality: it's too simple. It's too freaking easy and simple. We are complex, intelligent, smart people—we don't like bumper stickers.

Here's a sentence from the first paragraph of step ten in the Big Book. Here's how to live from now on. "Continue to watch for selfishness, dishonesty, resentment and fear. When these crop up, we ask God at once to remove them." That's it for the day. You got it?

Then another phenomenon comes along. If we have a vision as was described in the promises and we continue to work on it, it will expand. We will be much more controlled by our spiritual side than by our ego. Part of us loves it, and part of us hates it. This is very threatening to that part of us that controlled our lives until we got to AA.

The ego is going to come up with different techniques of talking to us. One of the most common is, *Mary, you know that "spiritual breakthrough" you had? The big light, the glimpse—you suddenly knew God's doing it? That was probably indigestion. Do you remember what you ate that day? A lot of people see stuff like that after a lot of hamburger and sauerkraut...* In other words, doubt is one of the greatest weapons to the spiritual progress.

I swear, about two months ago, I got up one day and I said, *Everything you know is a lie. All of AA is a lie. Why do you believe it? Where did that come from?* I was just standing there shaving. *This is your friend talking; I'm just trying to warn you all of that is a lie. Do you see God? Do you see any of this stuff? You can't be falling for this stuff still!*

Fortunately I just dismissed it, but if you hang in long enough and give those voices an audience, they'll take over again. They'll take over, and you'll be back checking the screen to see what you should do next. So I throw that out because I remember that so vividly, and it works something like this:

OK, we're inventorying. I'm changing this, I'm doing that. And it will just come in. It's you, so it doesn't have to really sneak in. It's already there.

It will just say, *Goddamn, look, look! Big trouble up there! Look! What?*

Made you look. Made you look. Made you look. Anything to get you to look up there. *The stock market went down 400 points. You're going to be broke in a week. Look.*

That's why we need each other and this program to maintain

and continue to develop the glimpse that we've been given. We have some beautiful language in the Big Book, and I just want to read these three.

We've ceased fighting anyone or anything. How's that for a new plan? Does that look anything like your old plan? We've ceased fighting anyone or anything. That means anything can happen and that's fine with you. Do you ever think you'd get there?

Wait a minute. You mean I just leave the world untouched?

Yeah.

Isn't it important for the world to know my opinion?

No.

Shouldn't I be looking at it and seeing what I can straighten out?

No.

We've ceased fighting anyone or anything. Now we want to contribute to the world, we want to change the world. This is how you change it. There can't be peace in the world till we're at peace with ourselves. We have to find inner peace—that is what this is all about. Then it will just happen. We will just spread peace wherever we go. It's very contagious; it is a program of attraction, not a program of jamming something down your throat. Well, we've got three million people who've been attracted just from the message these two guys started—that's pretty powerful stuff. Let's stay in the booth instead of on the screen. Let's just continue in here.

Now it's describing what spirituality looks like. It's talking specifically about drinking, but this applies to all other situations. **We've been placed in a position of neutrality.** What a place. I'm neutral. I am just unaffected; I'm neutral. The problem has been removed. That is the difference: problems aren't solved, they're removed. We took forgiveness and we made amends, and it cleaned the slides. And the problems on the slides were removed.

When the problem was removed, the light shone through. I made the problem—all we did was undo my work, and that's what we all do. It's always going to come back to me: continue to take personal inventory, and when I'm wrong, promptly admit it. When

I find something going wrong, I admit it and I ask God to remove it.

Then we have the wonderful sentence, "**We have a daily reprieve contingent on the maintenance of our booth (spiritual condition).**" As long as we are maintaining this cleansing of the slides, the light will shine, and we will enjoy our lives. It is all in here, but part of us is going to keep telling ourselves, *Hey, hey!* And it will be back in action. *There's a bunch of stuff that needs to be fixed.* This step is setting us up for the rest of our sobriety with looking at only ourselves.

Now, the Twelve and Twelve is also brilliant on this step, in my opinion. In the Twelve and Twelve is the sentence that people use all the time, which is, *How do you know if something's wrong in the booth?* Here's how you know. If something disturbs you no matter what the cause, there's something wrong in the booth.

That's paraphrasing the Twelve and Twelve. If something disturbs you, no matter what it is, there's something wrong with you. Now see, that is entirely in harmony with everything we've been saying. Problem? It's in the booth. You go, *Gee whiz, what about them? What about them?* We want to protect ourselves. *He did that, and that happened, and that happened. What is wrong with me?*

You're disturbed. That's what's wrong.

How do you get undisturbed? That's why I love the Twelve and Twelve. It's a four-point plan.

One: self-restraint. That is the great gift to pray for. Self-restraint. Things happen—do nothing. Some people call it counting to ten; you can call it whatever you want to call it. Do nothing.

My boss said to me, *This memo sucks.*

It hurt me so deeply I said, *I quit!*

The words are now crossing the office, but they haven't got to his ears yet, and I want to get them back because I need this job. With self-restraint I say, *OK, I'll look at it.* That's number one.

A friend of mine, Ed, whose memorial service I went to last week, used to say he lets five people be wrong ahead of time when he's going to work, which is a spiritual cushion against the world.

Five jerks can do anything they want today, and I'm giving them permission. There was another guy who would have Thursday be Traffic Day—everybody can drive anyway they want. *Fine, fine. Yeah, cut in! That was my spot, but you take it.*

When you do that, you see, *Goddarn, I didn't get upset all day. This is funny watching all these clowns out here.* That's because the ego wasn't involved, and there's probably a better spot right up around the corner. That is self-restraint, which allows the rest of the three things to take place. Without self-restraint, we blow up, and it's over.

The second is an honest analysis of what's wrong. I use someone else. I call up somebody and say, *How are you?* It only takes a minute or so. *This happened. A guy said that, I said that. Now I really feel terrible.* Then I get my feedback.

He said, *Well, you're totally wrong. You're reading the situation wrong. You're absolutely 100 percent wrong. Go make an amend.*

I go make the amend, and I'm back to undisturbed.

The goal is to always to get back to undisturbed. This is the new goal for the day; it used to be "make a lot of money." Used to be "get a promotion." Now we're in the world of the spirit, undisturbed. If you go through the day undisturbed, you win. We have new scoring system. *You undisturbed? Hey, put a check mark up there! You're ahead!*

That's all we wanted anyway. That's all we ever wanted—peace of mind, to get undisturbed. What if it's another person I called up? I tell a story about my boss, and my friend says, *Wow, your boss is completely out of line. You don't have anything to do with that. That is outrageous, outrageous behavior. Forgive him.* Where do we end up? Undisturbed. I either made an amend or I forgave, because the game isn't to win. There's no competition; there's nobody to roll over. I'm just working in the booth. I'm just getting that straightened out. We have to get rid of a lot of other rules that we had on how to handle a million different situations.

This is totally foreign, so we're going to make mistakes. So practice. We continue this step for the rest of our lives trying to get better and better and better at not only not getting disturbed, but if we do, getting undisturbed very quickly. As you look back on a year, maybe you only got very angry twice.

Do you know what a change that is for all of us? To look back and say, *Last year I only got really angry twice.* Most of us were in anger management before we even showed up here. We spent half our time angry. Angry at what? At that mess up there that we created. We were going to stay angry till we hit the grave or until we started changing inside. When it says it's the world of the spirit, that's what it means.

You see how many areas we're going to have to give up trying to control? Man, I'll tell you, this is not a pleasant process, but it's a jackpot. It is an absolute win-win, more winning, more winning. When we go to the last couple of steps, you'll see that now we want to really open the channel and see how much light we can get before the game's over.

How bright can we get that light with what time we have left?

11

One Problem and
One Solution

NOW WE JUST about wrapped up the history last week, as far as the stuff that is in the history books. The historical figures have pretty well faded into the past. There are only two left to talk about. Bill didn't have any children. He and Lois tried, but they ended up not having any children; there are no heirs over on that side. Dr. Bob had two children; a daughter, Sue, and a son also named Bob, but called "Smitty." Sue, ended up running off to get married with one of the first guys to get sober in Akron, Ernie Galbraith, AA number four, much to the chagrin of those around there. He was staying in their house—that is really taking advantage of your sponsor, when you take off with his daughter. We were doing outrageous things from day one, which is why sponsors don't look surprised when you tell them some outrageous thing, because it's already happened or they've done it.

Sue eventually re-married her childhood sweetheart, Ray Windows. She passed away in 2002 and was survived by her two sons. A lot of people around here may have met Smitty, because of all things he ended up in Al-Anon, having married an alcoholic. That brought him into the fellowship through a different door than his father. The two of them collaborated on a book, "The Children of the Healer: The Story of Dr. Bob's Kids." It's very interesting. Smitty talked about his own life; he was a B-24 pilot in WWII, a very successful businessman, and he re-married after his wife died. A lot of us met his wife, but they hadn't been married but for about a year when he died in 2004. An interesting thing I noted when I read their book was the beginning of Sue's story. She took almost the entire first page to let everybody know that Bill Wilson got too much credit, compared to Dr. Bob. It is funny how that Akron perspective on things continued. It just continued over the years.

Henrietta Sieberling felt the same way. Anything that she wrote or was quoted on, just made it clear that there was too much publicity that went to New York. To this day, there is still the tension on the two approaches to AA.

You have seen the circle and the triangle. Then you know that the triangle is labeled, "Recovery, Unity, and Service," which are the three legacies of Alcoholics Anonymous. We have talked about the steps, which are Recovery. We talked about the traditions, which are Unity. But we haven't really talked about the Service side of Alcoholics Anonymous much.

When you go back to the very beginning, Alcoholics Anonymous was pretty much run by Doctor Bob, Bill Wilson and the Alcoholic Foundation Board.

If you recall, Bill set up the foundation after Rockefeller wouldn't give him any money, because he thought money would ruin AA. Bill said, *Very interesting, but I want to raise money.* He got the Foundation Board and set out to use them to raise money. From the very beginning, Bill wanted to make sure that there were more non-alcoholics on the board than alcoholics. They hired a law firm to write the bylaws of the original Board. The lawyers had a very hard time figuring out how to put in the legal document the definition of an alcoholic. In other words, how do you explain being an alcoholic *legally*? They really wrestled with that. They ended up with three non-alcoholics and two alcoholics. One of the alcoholics on the Board got drunk and had to be replaced. That started the thing, *Well, we better keep the number of non-alcoholics in greater numbers than the alcoholics.* It became a sore spot with Bill, as he felt AA had matured and he wanted to change the majority over to the alcoholics.

That Board was increased a couple of times, up to nine members. Then in 1954, the Foundation was over, and we created the General Service Board. Since that time, that has been the entity that is mainly in charge of our service.

In 1955, it was a big thing for Bill and the old-timers. At the St. Louis Convention, Bill knew that eventually AA had to govern itself, that all the drunks coming in had to be in charge of their own fellowship. Up until then, they would just run to Bill: *What do we do about this? What do we do about that?* He knew he would die eventually—Doctor Bob already had died –so they had a formal passing on in 1955 of the three legacies over to the Fellowship itself. The General Service Conference became the Conscience and Director of the organization that you and I belong to.

In 1962, the General Service Conference adopted Bill's manuscript on the Twelve Concepts, which give instructions to the delegates and the board as to what principles they should follow in managing the affairs of Alcoholics Anonymous. The interesting thing is, that manuscript adopted by the General Service Conference is the only official publication in AA with a byline—*By Bill W.*

Not until 1971, in spite of transferring everything over, could we resist asking Bill's opinion on everything. He was still alive and showing up, and he dropped in the office once in a while. It was really difficult. Finally in 1971, when he passed on, we started running our own show. In the back of the Big Book—just about the last page—are the Twelve Concepts. They basically describe where the authority in the fellowship is. They talk about the fact that the GSC is our voice and conscience and then they establish certain rights: the right to make decisions, the right of appeal, and the right to participate.

That means we all get to participate as much as we want, and when decisions are made, they can be appealed. The Concepts are very important, and the final one says that power should never be centralized in one little group or one person. That's a very important concept.

Right now, managing our affairs are twenty-one trustees; Bill was able in 1966 to get the majority of the trustees to be alcoholic. And now there are fourteen alcoholics and seven non-alcoholics that constitute our board of trustees. In addition to them, we have ninety-three delegates from the US and Canada in ninety-three Areas in those two countries. If problems are coming up and we want to make sure New York and the annual General Service Conference hears about them and deals with them or at least thinks about them, there is a process in place. We have our intergroup representative, and we attend meetings and find out what is going on in other groups. You will see when we get into some of the issues that AA service has had to deal with, that it is really important to participate in this.

We also have the General Service Office and the employees in the New York Office. There are eleven employees in that office, and each one of them has an office and a specific area of responsibility, like literature, conferences, dealing with people overseas, dealing with the professionals, and dealing with prisons and jails. In the absolute tradition of AA, every two years they pick up all their crap and move over to the office next to them and take over those responsibilities. Nobody gets to be in charge. With that expertise, if something happens to one of them, there are other people there that know how that job is done while they break in somebody new. It's a fascinating thing in New York—they just switched offices last month. If you had been up there, you would have seen Moving Day. The delegates have a term of two years, the trustees are now two consecutive three year terms and the GSO staff rotates every two years.

I did some research and looked at some of the issues just so you know what has come up. These are some that I've decided to take a look at. One of them was reaching out. Part of AA's job is to carry the message to other alcoholics. The first example of reaching out goes all the way back to the very beginning when Catholics were having a hard time joining Alcoholics Anonymous. Do you remember that story from back in Akron? They came down from Cleveland, and the church said, *Well, if you are going to the Oxford Group, we are going to excommunicate you.* Clarence decided to start a meeting outside and not call up the Oxford Group, and they were accommodated. Since that time they have made special efforts to reach out to people of color, women, disabled people and illiterate people. That became an important element. How do we help a person who can't even read our literature? What can we do to help that alcoholic stay sober? There are pamphlets for gays, Indians, young people and old people. (They are talking about the old alcoholics that can't believe that they have the problem; getting them to surrender and try AA is very difficult.) There is outreach for people in the military, or in jails and prisons. They would have meetings and they would come up with, *This seems like a good idea. This is how we can go to jails*, so our institutions committees were formed. This is the kind of stuff that gets deliberated.

The next thing was the professionals. Now we didn't have to worry about professionals until the 1970s when federal laws were passed making alcoholism a disease. That didn't bring the professionals in. It happened when it was covered by insurance. That brought the professionals in because now you could make money treating drunks. Up until then you didn't want them in your office. They never paid their bills. Who wanted to help them? Now with insurance coverage, other people advised new alcoholics on how to stay sober. Sometimes this happened in conflict to what they heard when they eventually arrived at Alcoholics Anonymous, so we had an outreach program so that AA could go and talk to professionals and make them more aware of what AA was doing.

Then we ran into the treatment center that said, *Jeez the best counselors would be AA members.* When that first happened—I don't know if some of you were around then—it was, *He is a two-hatter.* That was the term that was being used. *He is a traitor to carrying the message for nothing. He is being paid to carry that message.*

They finally resolved that he wasn't Twelve-Stepping, and he wasn't carrying the message. He was helping the person get through detox and educating them about the disease and getting them ready to come to Alcoholic Anonymous. Now many of us work in the treatment facilities with no problems whatsoever and no stigma attached.

We ran into the first time that judges started sending people to AA. I couldn't believe it. A guy came in with a sheet of paper. When it is the first sheet of paper that you've ever seen at an AA meeting, you go, *We don't sign papers. We've never signed one before, and I'm not starting tonight.*

I think I am capturing the essence of every AA group. *We don't do it that way.* We had to go through the process of educating all the AA groups and talking with judges, and things have smoothed out. Now it's not a major event. Then we had the treatment centers taking people through the steps in treatment. Then they come out and have a sponsor and they go, *Oh, no, the treatment center told us that's not the way to do that at all.* We had to work out that kind of problem. Other problems were about conflicting advice to newcomers, pills, and outside experts. The earliest one that I remember is the Rand Report from the Rand Think Tank up in Washington; they concluded that AA didn't know what they were doing, that we really ought to be taking alcoholics and teaching them how to drink. We had to respond to these various things.

I remember the Sobells were two psychologists from Canada. All of a sudden, they announced that they had been treating alcoholics for years with their aversion therapy and had gotten hundreds of people sober. This was the only time where there had been great big numbers, and everybody went *Wow, what is this?* It stayed that way for a number of years until two more psychologists studied the follow-up: nobody was sober. It turns out they had been doing their research by calling the alcoholic asking how they were doing.

I'm doing great!

OK! We have another success down there in Utah!

Then we went through the types of groups. Within AA itself, people started smaller groups: a women's group or a men's group or a gays' group. In other words, it had nothing to do with having a different disease. It is just that we find comfort in getting to people who are similar to us. We've used that with women, old people, young people, pilots, lawyers and doctors. I find them very useful when you are new, but then it is time to get into mainstream AA, where there is one of everything in the room and not just a table that looks just like you. There, all you get is the same perspective that you have. There are no old housewives telling Marine Colonels they are full of crap at a military meeting. *Well, you may fly the plane well, but you are stupid.*

If a treatment center wants to offer a meeting-type situation, sometimes we call that a meeting. We take a meeting to a treatment center so that the people in there can hear what a meeting sounds like and can get sponsors, but it is not a group. Nobody belongs to it. The other thing was the dual-purpose meetings. Those started up as we got an increase in dual addiction. People said, *You know, I would be more comfortable just meeting with other people who are dually addicted.* Those groups started up, but the General Service Conference took a look at that and said, *Great, I hope it helps you, but we aren't going to list you as an AA group. That is not AA.* It was felt (very wisely) that the dual-purpose meetings would start broadening AA and weaken the identification that is so necessary.

There is also still a problem—and we've never really been able to completely address it—of drug addicts who choose to attend closed AA meetings in spite of knowing what the traditions are because there is nobody in charge. You can't *not* allow that. There are no rules in AA. That continues to be a problem across the country.

Then we have AA's finances—self-supporting. Of course they declined outside contributions from the very beginning, even though it was contrary to Bill's plan. They tried to make AA self-supporting, meaning from you and me. In 1964, when I came in, they passed the word that the General Service Office could function if every member of AA would donate a dollar a year, and they didn't get it. They had to get some of the income from Big Book sales. A dollar a year? When they ask groups if we can increase your donation, that's what they are talking about. They are trying to make us self-supporting, not off of selling books. As we got more successful with the Big Book (1 million, 5 million copies), suddenly non-members of AA are buying more literature than AA members, and our income—if you really get technical—is coming from outsiders. It wasn't a member buying a Big Book. It was a treatment center or a library. That created more urgency in upping the ante that comes from you and me. I would still say the average donation at an AA meeting—for all the coffee you can drink and all the spiritual advice you can get and the wonderful fellowship and camaraderie—is about one-fourth of what it costs for a cup of coffee at Starbucks. When they ask if we could put a little more in the collection, don't be embarrassed to put two dollars in. That's all I am saying. I am trying to share where they are. Bill had this saying when I was new. He said, *Drunks will buy the bar a round of drinks when they are drinking. They will set up Madison Square Garden. When they get sober, they are tight as the bark on a tree.*

Anyway the individual limit one could donate to AA went from $100 to $1,000. [*The current annual individual limit is $3,000 and a one time bequest is $5,000. –Ed.*] Lois wanted to donate Stepping Stones; they turned it down. They said, *No, we aren't going to take that and get the income off of that.* It became a state historical place.

I want to mention our magazine, the Grapevine. The Grapevine started out as a little tiny newsletter and has become one of the great magazines where people could contribute stories and share their experiences in AA. It was a very powerful thing. A man outside of Chicago just celebrated his sixtieth anniversary. I sent him a card. His name is Paul M. I used to wait for the Grapevine that would have a Paul M. story in it where he would discuss some principle in AA. He is such a good writer. It really was exciting. There is a general feeling across the fellowship that, as the years have gone on, while Grapevine became more diverse, it backed off on really focusing on God. The God banner just seemed less than it used to be and it was more of a reflection, perhaps, of our culture. *The country doesn't want to hear that much about God, so we won't put it in there; it might offend somebody.* Now that's just a few people's opinion. I'm sure there are other ways of looking at this.

That was the last thing I was going to talk about in terms of the structure and the history of AA. Now we are just left with the eleventh step: "Sought through prayer and meditation to improve our conscious contact with God as we understood Him, praying only for knowledge of his will for us and the power to carry that out." Quite a mouthful. At some point in telling stories, I told you about one of my heroes, Chuck C, Chuck Chamberlain. His assessment as he got older was, *For all human beings, there is only one problem, and that includes all problems. There is only one solution, and that includes all solutions. The problem is conscious separation from God.*

Our awareness—before we get working on these steps—tells us that we exist separate from God. I don't know if you relate to that, but it was like, *Yeah, but… I'm over here. I'm not in the big circle of everything. I'm over here.* That's what conscious separation is, and it exists because of our story. We put together all of the slides, and God isn't in them. So, whenever we look at the world that we created, we see ourselves at the center, just like in a dream. We become the center of our own lives, which causes terrible problems, because it's *us against them.* It's, *I'm the only one I can rely on. I have to be strong. The world is unfair.* It's so overpowering and it's all caused by conscious separation.

What is this eleventh step? "Sought to improve our conscious contact." No more separation. Conscious contact. Now, we're in touch with a different world. Instead of being *apart from*, we're *a part of.* Instead of living apart from everything, I become part of something. That begins with starting to be part of AA. You start to like it and think, *I'm really part of AA. It is the only thing I am a part of.* And then as I worked the steps and went through the changing of the old ideas, our slides, the picture on the screen started changing. It became apparent that the Creator is the center, and I'm just one of the guys on the bus. It took a lot of pressure off. I wasn't in charge of anything. I'm just supposed to show up, have a cup of coffee, listen to the speaker, and enjoy it. My top job is to enjoy life. We absolutely insist on enjoying life.

Of course, the ego has not given up. We've made a lot of progress in squashing that guy down, erasing old ideas. And he sees prayer and meditation and he immediately comes up. I don't know about you all, but as soon as somebody said "prayer and meditation," I said, *That doesn't work*. I had never tried it, but I said, *It doesn't work. Why should I try something that doesn't work?*

Bill uses a sentence that I've always loved. He said, "We are the same as a scientist who refuses to perform a certain experiment lest it prove his pet theory wrong." Part of us doesn't want to try prayer and meditation out of fear that it might work and make us look like a jerk. *Hey, I've been wrong all these years. This stuff really works.* Now, isn't that silly that we could cut off our nose to spite our face and not give this a fair shake? All of this is designed to further erase our old ideas and move closer to the light so that it can shine through.

Then we have, "Praying only for knowledge of His will for us and the power to carry that out." Many people, when they see that, think, *Well, I'd like to do that, but I also want to pray for my uncle and world peace and starving people.* There are all these causes that we want to pray for and yet the step suggests, "Praying only for knowledge of His will for us and the power to carry that out."

This is a remarkable change in the traditional way of looking at prayer: praying only for knowledge of His will for us and the power to carry that out. The purpose of the whole program is to have an awakening. If we go back to "The Varieties of Religious Experience," the author said the greatest contribution that has ever been made to the human race are awakened people. That contributes more to the world than anything. It is a much higher goal than a limited target. A limited target—how is the target of our prayer chosen? By my ego—I think of one thing that ought to be different. I want this person to get well … or maybe they are not supposed to get well. However, maybe they are supposed to learn some lessons from further sickness. In other words, we aren't in charge of everything.

Bill makes this point over and over that when we're doing that, we are simply looking at the big screen and deciding what's wrong. We're working up there instead of in here. It may sound unkind, but it really isn't. Of course, we want all these things to turn out a certain way. But the best way we can contribute to all of that is to allow more light to come through us. That's the greatest contribution that we can make. That's why we pray only for knowledge of His will for us and the power to carry that out. If we focus on that, then we're back in our slide booth working only on the slides in there and not keeping track of what's going on in the world. If we want to change the world that we're living in, this is where we work—on our collection of slides.

I estimate that the average person has around 10,000 or 15,000 slides. We have opinions on everything. We have memories of experiences. Each day, we look around going, *That's wrong, that's right. I hate that.* This probably happens a thousand times a day, and we don't even know it. It causes us a great deal of pain until we stop fixing the screen and decide to stay in here. That's when we inventory and start bringing them up to get them erased, so that only light shines through. That's a long-term project, but as the results come in, it looks something like the prayer of St. Francis. We reach in and take out the hatred slide, and we allow the program to erase it. We start focusing on our Higher Power, and what shines through is Love. It came out of us.

This is what is inside of us. When you read the prayer of St. Francis, he is describing this. He is describing the powers that are inside of us and what happens when the barriers to them are released. He is describing you. This is who you really are. Your essence is Love. Hatred is what we got by watching this stuff, but *that* isn't who you are. That's the story that we create. "Where there is hatred, I bring Love. Where there is wrong..."

Remember when we looked at all the wrong in the world? *Look at that. That's wrong, that's wrong, you are wrong, you wronged me.* Then we clear this off, and what comes out is forgiveness. That comes out naturally. *Oh, somebody wronged me. Well, they are probably messed up. I'll pray for them. That's fine.* It is a whole different thing. You can see we are so free as these events are happening. Everything is screwed up—absolute discord. Then we work on that; harmony comes out. This is what is inside already. This isn't anything that we learn. It is there. This is the true nature of our spiritual selves. We are not learning how to be loving; we are loving. It's just blocked by this stuff we have been creating up there.

Where there is error, we bring truth. Truth comes intuitively. It suddenly is revealed. We didn't figure out. We didn't study it in the Big Book. We didn't do anything. We just got error washed and washed and what was left was truth coming out. Where there is doubt, and so we get that to disappear, faith automatically appears. We already have it. You see how different a view of everything this is? That where there is despair. *Oh my God, it is the end of the world.* Well, let's not play that one anymore. Let's just wipe it.

Hope springs eternal, just out it comes. It's already there. That's the wonderful gift that we are getting here—the awareness that is already inside if we do this work. "Where there are shadows, I bring light." There is the light. We don't go get it and bring it. It shines. You watch people in this program and follow them—at the beginning, they might say, *Yeah, I can't believe my sponsor wants me to go to New York and make a freaking amend.* Then they start glowing. Because they went up there and erased an old hatred slide. You start seeing them at meetings, always happy.

Finally, "Where there is sadness, I bring joy." Bill said the whole theme of AA is the joy of living. Why do people become joyful? Because they got sadness out of the way. It is such a different way of looking at all of this. St. Francis went through hell to get to this point, where his awareness showed all of this. When you see a picture of him, birds are sitting on his shoulder, and deer are coming out of the woods, just to stand near him. What is that? I would say, in AA vernacular, *That is a program of attraction.*

You don't come in here to get beaten to do these things. You go, *That really happens? Does that really happen?* Then we see it happening in people. That is called the program of attraction. Then he goes on, and it is in self-forgetting that one finds. The way to really take care of yourself is to not take care of yourself. *I'm just going to leave that go.* Then everything is revealed to us. It is by forgiving that one is forgiven. It by dying that one wakens the life eternal.

What does dying mean? Clean slides. It's almost as if you're walking around without a past, a man without a country, a man without a past. *I can't even remember what I used to resent.* How would that be?

What's your biggest resentment?

Goddamn, I couldn't even remember. Where did it go? Somebody blotted it out. Goddamn, I wished I kept a record. I can't remember.

What a different way of looking at all of this. Sought through prayer and meditation to improve this contact that began at the end of the promises, when we said we suddenly realized that God is doing for us what we couldn't do for ourselves. The awareness was personal. It wasn't a theory. It wasn't, *Well, God's real to me because others tell me about it. No, that's not real; that's just book knowledge.* What we want in order for this to really work is for us to go, *Holy cow! I felt it myself. You mean this spiritual stuff works?*

I remember a couple of young people up in Washington, D.C., about eighteen or nineteen, and one of them was trying to talk to his buddy, who was brand new into the program. He summed it all up by looking him right in the eye and saying, *This spiritual crap works.*

You know something? That's the language of the heart. His buddy went, *It does?*

Before it changed me, I thought it was spiritual crap.

It stays that way until we do it. Then, we started having this experience and sought to improve our conscious contact.

For our story purposes, improving is getting another slide erased, getting another one erased. Now, the more that we do that, the more we will intuitively know how to handle things. We will bring an awareness and a knowledge to the situation that we didn't have before. We're going to contribute much more to every situation than we did in the past. And none of it is going to happen by learning anything. It's all going to happen by erasing what we know. Isn't that ironic? *Oh, you know all about that? Come here... Now you don't.*

We're not talking about knowledge about how to work a computer or how to do your job. We're talking about how the world works, your personal story about the world, your editorializing. That's what we're talking about here, because that is where all our problems are.

As we said earlier, our problems are of our own making. Who made all these lousy slides?

Oh, I did. Yeah, every one in there I made, and I made it by thinking.

That's how we create them.

Come to think of it, what that guy did was really bad. As a matter of fact, the more I think about it, it's outrageous what he did. I'm going to think about it all night. I'm going to move it up to kill him.

So, thinking has to be out, and that's where prayer and meditation come in. We're trying to go into a state where thinking is sitting on the outside, not screwing everything up. Thinking is the ego saying, *Prayer and meditation isn't going to work. You don't want to try that. You'd look silly. What if somebody came in the room and you had your eyes closed? They'd go, "Look at Larry!" and laugh.* That's the ego trying to talk us out of doing this.

You'll look bad. It's not going to work. Remember you tried it once when you were fifteen. Nothing happened. That's enough proof for me.

As I inventoried my ideas to get rid of them, I found that most of them were put together by the time I was fifteen. I was forty. They governed my life, and I was reluctant to get rid of them, even though they produced terrible results. Look if you keep doing that, you are always going to feel sick.

I know, but it's me. It's the real me, I would hate to… That is the pride trying to hold on to the way you thought things should be or are—your evaluation of the situation. The hardest thing for self-centered people to give up is there judgment about things. When we give that up and go through this process, we see what the situation looks like from God's perspective. It is entirely different.

12

A Wonderful World

WE'VE COME TO the last step. If you recall from chapter one, we snuck ahead to the end of the book to see how it ends, so that we would know what we were doing the whole time. And here is where we get to the jackpot—that spiritual awakening.

Having had a spiritual awakening as the result of these steps, we tried to carry this message to others and practice these principles in all our affairs.

It has been my experience that part of a spiritual experience is the irresistible desire to pass it on. You can just have three months and still be telling somebody with one week, *Let me tell you! Let me tell you!* We run over. We don't know what we are going to tell them, but boy, we're excited. That's the contagious nature of spirituality, and we talk about it all the time. You have to give it away in order to keep it.

Well, it's almost like we don't have to talk about it, because it's part of the deal. In the '70s—I don't see this much anymore—when treatment centers were really big, somebody would get to two years and inevitably start talking about passing it on.

You'd go, *Well, how is it going?*

You know what I'm thinking? I'm thinking of becoming an alcohol counselor. This desire was part of passing it on.

We'd suggest, *Hang with it for about six months. It'll probably go away*. And it generally did.

That enthusiasm and the exuberance that we have to share this is almost irresistible, and that's why this is so much fun for me. It's to just get up and try to pass on all the wonderful things that have happened to me to those of you that are just getting here.

When we go back and take a look at our Big Book now that we're operating on a frequency of awakening, we will find lots of sentences that talk about it. Maybe we kind of slid by them when we were going through it. I wrote down some of them.

"We may have been granted a glimpse of that ultimate reality, which is God's Kingdom." That's quite a statement. It's a glimpse. That's what breaking through the ego is. That's what cleaning those slides off is—a glimpse. A glimpse is enough to get us to want more and to see it more clearly and to have a better view.

"We have found much of heaven and we have been rocketed into a fourth dimension of existence of which we had not even dreamed" (The Big Book, page 25).

These are amazing sentences. They're just scattered throughout the Big Book. From the beginning of the Big Book (page 25): "The central fact of our lives today is the absolute certainty that our Creator has entered into our hearts and lives in a way which is indeed miraculous." *The absolute certainty.*

This is the difference between knowing about some Higher Power and experiencing it. You go, *Wow, that's what they're talking about, and it just happened to me.* This is why AA is so successful and so much fun. It's because that's what we're passing on. It's how to have that happen to you.

"We found the Great Reality deep down within us" (The Big Book, page 55).

"When we drew near to Him He disclosed Himself to us!" (The Big Book, page 57).

"We have entered the world of the Spirit" (The Big Book, page 84).

"We feel we are on the Broad Highway, walking hand in hand

with the Spirit of the Universe" (The Big Book, page 75). Now, what a feeling that is. I'm walking hand in hand. I'm a little child, and I have my hand in my Father's hand, and we're going to walk that way forever.

It's the perfect picture, except for my ego saying, *Yeah, this is great, but I look like a wimp. Look at everybody staring at me holding onto somebody's hand instead of handling all this on my own.* There is the internal struggle. We're given the perfect deal, and we decide to improve on it. That's what we mean when we take it back. People during the week will say, *Well, I decided to do today on my own. I've been to four meetings to recover from it, but I seem to be doing a little bit better.*

We see this circle, this cycle where we started and ended. The steps really could be put in a circle or on a piano as piano keys. We "play" different steps to stay in harmony with the situation that we're encountering in that moment. They become an integral part of us, and these are the new ways of relating to the world.

We used the analogy of, "We are a spiritual being having a human experience." Most people seemed to like that. It helps to understand what's going on. Now, in order to do that, we have to be given a mind and awareness so that we can *experience* the human experience. Part of that awareness is the ability to think about things other than what's going on; we call that awareness of our ego.

We are having a human experience, which was fully intended, but we're also editorializing on it as it happens and categorizing it as pretty bad. *That was pretty bad, what happened to me when I was six.* Events just happened, but we filed them away as pretty bad. *God never should have allowed that to happen.* We built a story, starting around age three or four—the first time we said, "Mine." Then we just kept building it.

Now, the more we build this story (and we're encouraged to do so, because everybody else on the planet is doing that), the more difficult it is to get out of it. That's why we talked about how lucky we are and what a small percentage of the people in the middle of their stories ever have a chance to break out. As the years go on, the story thickens. It becomes a place where we can hide. In the beginning, it seemed like it was good protection. We could hide in our shell. Most of us became loners, and we felt safe in there. Other stuff is going on, but we could go isolate ourselves and think about things. Remember that—that's important. You can't just go in there. You got to go in there and think about things. *Man, the more I think about it, it's crappier than I thought. It's much worse than I thought yesterday. I'm going to think about it some more.* There are more ramifications to this, and I'm building a thicker and thicker shell.

Now, this shell becomes almost like a bird's eggshell. In order to survive and to not die in that shell, that little bird has to break out of there. That has to be one heck of a struggle, especially if the shell is a little thicker than it should have been or the bird is a little weaker. Now, most people never get a shot at this. They just assume, *This is all there is, and I'm going to make the best of existing in here with all of my ideas that are scaring the hell out of me. I go to therapy, I go read books, I go everywhere, but I never get out of there. I can make it.* It's like getting an interior decorator for your prison cell. *This really looks nice! It looks a lot better than it did last week. I'm still in there, though, and I know it. I know that there is supposed to be something more than this. I also miss something: how it was before I built this prison to hide in.*

We've been talking about this in terms of slides. You can use any analogy, but that becomes the reality that we live in. We make it so bad that the only way to live there is to drink. At least drinking makes it seem like it's better. But when we sober up, it's worse. It's much worse!

This is sort of like the human condition. Those of us that are lucky enough—those of us that are in the small, minute 10 percent of alcoholics who find AA—are given a chance to bust through that shell, to actually crack our own ego and see beyond it. Now, the ego is telling us there isn't anything beyond it. *This is all there is.* How often have we been told that? *This is all there is. Stop talking about that. You're not in a shell. You're just screwed up. Get a therapist and get with it.*

We come in here, and here's the amazing part. The people in here have done it, and they were exactly in the same place we were. They were alcoholics. When we met them and they told us their stories, we cemented with that bond of identification that we talked about during primary purpose. That's what connected me to trying this. I suddenly went, *That guy got out, and he also knows what it feels like to be in here.*

That was amazing—the first time I heard somebody talk like he was reading my mind. He hid vodka in the toilet just like I did! I couldn't believe it. Then the stories he made up—they were the stories I made up. It was almost like, *Did my sponsor brief this guy ahead of time to give a talk like that so that I would see?* We've all had that happen, where we suddenly identify and realize we're in the right place. So we decide to try something that looks absolutely weird.

When we look at these Twelve Steps from an intellectual perspective, it looks like hogwash. Because we're trying to reason with them. We're trying to make sense out of them intellectually. We're trying to understand the steps. We aren't in that world. We're moving to the world of the spirit that the tenth step talked about, and we don't use the same language. The trick to the steps is to *do* them on faith! A lot of us call it *taking action in something we don't believe in.* I didn't believe in them, but I knew if I didn't do them, my sponsor might hurt me. That's my story.

Another thing is peer pressure. *Well, everybody else is doing it. I'm going to look bad.* Even the ego tricks itself. *I'm going to look bad if I don't do them*—so now we're doing something to get the ego, and he didn't even realize it. But for whatever reason, we suddenly find the magic word coming into our vocabulary: "willing." I become *willing*. Willing means to set aside my judgment in favor of someone I chose—my sponsor or the group or the collective wisdom of Alcoholics Anonymous—and allowed that to be superior to my intellect and my decisions about how my life should go. That is a huge step. This is the place where it happens.

You can see how lucky we are to hit bottom. Now, hitting bottom is the beginning of the effort to get out. That motivates us. Everyone's story is different. That is the point at which the journey down stops. That's the bottom floor. Now, we're going to go the other way—not by our own knowledge or our own resources, but by the power of the program, our sponsors, and our newfound Higher Power. We begin the process of breaking out.

I love to think of the Twelve Steps as the process of breaking out. *OK, gang, we're planning a break out tonight! Let's meet in an anonymous meeting, not use our names, and we'll plan the breakout! It's like we're sneaking up on our egos, tricking them with diversionary tactics, and breaking out.* Because once you do break out a little bit and get a taste of that light, it becomes irresistible. We just want more. This is where we start.

About a couple of years ago, I was thinking about how I tricked myself—how everybody does. They call life a game. They call it an illusion, a play. Here's a crazy little poem that makes me laugh at myself: "'Where shall I hide,' I said, 'where I will never find me?' I know. I'll pretend that I'm not me nor you nor he. I'll hide in a story and pretend that it's real. Oh, boy, what a joke on me." I love that last line. "Oh, boy, what a joke on me."

It's amazing. When I look at some of the stuff I got rid of, I think, *I can't believe that was my philosophy. I can't believe this was my way of living. Me—nice, smart guy? This is crap.* But I was proud of it. Oh, well.

We come to see how everything goes around, how there are two sides to everything. We start realizing we're going to be happy, then we're going to be sad, and then we're going to be happy, and then we're going to be sad. Everything is very cyclical, because if there weren't both of them, neither one could exist. There can't be sadness without happiness. I think that's what Einstein means about relativity. In order to be a down, there has to be an up. In order to have black, there has to be a white. There can't just be white, because it wouldn't be in relation to anything, and we wouldn't call it anything.

That's why we have all these things: life and death, birth and death, war and peace, up and down, in and out. When I breathe, I'm actually giving birth to a breath on the way in and saying good-bye to it on the way out. It's a very short lifespan. I breathe in: *Hey, how are you doing? Come on in. I need some oxygen!*

Don't worry, I'll take care of it.

Leaving already?

Yeah, I am.

Well, thanks for your help. You're taking the carbon dioxide out?

Yes, I am.

OK … Hi, welcome! Come on in.

Oops, sorry! I got to go.

…Oh, hi, come on in. Now, you may not do that when you're breathing, but you're not as crazy as I am.

When we see it that way—birth, death, birth, death—it's hardly a big deal. As soon as one ends, the other one starts, so we can't make a big deal out of anything. It's just the way it is. It's very cyclical.

Another balanced pair –I was thinking about it because they're part of us—is perfection and imperfection. We're all perfectionists. *Well, we ought to be doing it perfectly. You're not doing it right. You're too vague. It's too wishy-washy.* You hear it in here when we say, *You gotta get back to the basics.* The meaning is, *You're getting too watered down. You got to get back there.*

We were talking about that in the history of the tension between Akron and New York. We're using those because that's how we are. We have the same tension inside of us, so it's a wonderful way of looking at it. We had the Bible versus "anything goes," if you want to carry to that extreme. We look at it and we go, *Well, that's right. We got to go back to where everything is black and white.* There's that part of us that wants that rigidity, the conservative, everything in order.

Then you have no fun. *I want to get out and mess around for a while.* Then I go over here and I go, *This is more like it.* As soon as I get through, this side of me goes, *You should be ashamed of yourself. What's wrong with you?* Then I get a club and I go, "Can I have a little bit of fun?" "OK, go ahead. Sorry, I was only kidding." Bang, bang, bang. We just have to accept this and that, the yin and the yang.

We have the extreme moralism and the liberalism. We could phrase it this way: *Do you want to follow a co-founder who was faithful to his wife?*

Oh, yeah! You see, it's that simple. It's black and white. Well, if we did that, we wouldn't have any writings. Maybe one short letter. It looks like we're going to have to settle for following imperfect people. You're going to find that your sponsor is imperfect, and you're going to find your home group is imperfect. We're going to make stupid mistakes.

Oops, here comes the treasurer. What's the problem?

Oh, I ran off with the money.

All right, come on. We'll set up a payment plan. Welcome back.

I don't know what got into me. I don't know what happened.

What we want to do is not say, *Well, you ought to be ashamed of yourself.* Instead we say, *You know, I could have done that. I could have been in that spot if they left me with all the money. Who knows?* We see that in the whole nature of things, where it goes one way and then it goes another way.

The greatest cyclical thing that I like to talk about is where you and I are now, what happened in this wonderful AA journey. As you know, we hit a bottom, and now we're going the other way. Every year, we see things more brightly. It's just wonderful to see that. It really was something with a beginning and an end, then another beginning and then another end. To use a story, I'm going to steal two stories and make them into one. These two stories have been around since the beginning.

I'm going to call the story "The Prodigal Adam." It seems that Adam was in his father's kingdom, which was perfect. He just loved it, and his father loved him. He said, *This is your deal. This is it. Enjoy it for the rest of your life, and you'll be as happy as can be.* But his father was pretty smart. He had a little device that he could use to tell if people in the kingdom really appreciated it and were grateful for everything that was there. The little device was an apple. He just said, *The whole deal is yours, just don't eat that freaking apple over there, OK? It's just an apple. Just don't even touch it, OK?*

As it turns out, the vast majority of the people found that, yes, it was fun, but they wanted the apple. We have all of these wonderful things. Did any of you ever focus on the negative only? You have a wonderful life and you just sit around focusing on one little thing? I'm sure the people in that kingdom thought a lot about that apple. Finally they said, *I don't want to live here anymore. I'm getting out of here. I'm taking the apple. I'm gonna go create my own world where it'll be a lot fairer. I can do better than this.* Off we go. The prodigal sons and daughters are on their own doing better than that. *I can improve on that kingdom. I know I can.*

We hear these stories every night at speaker meetings. *My name is Mary. I'm an alcoholic and I had a nice little house. My parents were pretty nice, and then I decided that the reason I'm so unhappy was because they were so nice.* How about that? It's always got to be their fault.

They were too poor. They were too rich. I was so rich. I was alone all the time.

Oh, wow. That's so bad. I feel so sorry for you.

We start our story. They are all the same except for the details. One person's puking in a boat, and another is puking in an oxygen mask. One person is robbing this, and the next person is stealing that. It's all leading to a bad ending. Along the way, we know it is. We could see it coming. We know if we keep doing the same thing, we're going to keep getting the same results.

What do we do? *You know, tonight will be different. I'll just have two beers, maybe a hamburger, play one game of pool and go home to my family.* All right, so what happens? When he gets bailed out of jail, the whole family is there lecturing him. He goes, *I know, I know, I know, it's crazy. I promise that won't be happening anymore.* Then he tells himself, *I'm going to have just one beer and a ham sandwich, and then I'll come home to my family.* Then he's back in jail. No matter what we come up with, we go down and down and down.

Eventually, we see the four horsemen and worse. Finally, we get to what we call the bottom. If we're lucky, there's a hand of somebody else who was just there. They take our hand, and they start leading us out of the trap. We come back, and it's a very long journey, but it gets happier and brighter and more useful and more rewarding. Finally, at the end of the line, we make it back to the kingdom. They are so happy to see us.

Hey, how was it?

Oh, bad, bad, bad, bad. I had no idea how wonderful this place was. Oh, my God. I'm just taking it all in. I can't believe that I left here. Well, I know one thing. I'm a hundred times happier than I was before! It's just amazing. That trip itself made this 20 times better! I can't look at it. I'm looking at the colors. I'm looking at indigo. I've never seen it that bright. Wow, this is amazing.

The guy said, *Yeah, well, we've noticed that everybody who goes down to earth comes back twenty times happier than they were.*

Really?

Yeah, that's why there's that six-mile line over there trying to get back from earth.

No kidding?

Yeah. Yeah, it really does that. By the way, they changed it from apple to banana, just so you know.

How did that happen?

Well, isn't that the damnedest thing you ever thought of? God, that's just amazing. He starts to settle in and appreciate the fact that, from his old place where he loved to sit, he can see five galaxies. He can feel God's energy just surrounding him, and he's experiencing a peace that was beyond his wildest dreams. He just sat there in awe and ecstasy that something this wonderful could happen to him.

He just sat, contemplating it. He just sat breathing in and out. He said to himself, *I now know what they were talking about when they said it couldn't get any better than this. This is it.* Then he thinks, *Bananas? Why would they switch from apples to bananas? I don't like apples anymore if I can't eat them with my dentures. Bananas are perfect. Why would they pick that? Why would they do that to me?* Then we learn out of all of this that that's not as good as it gets. It's about to get twenty times better. We start another journey and another cycle.

That's my story, and I'm sticking to it. It captures the nature of life for me. When we understand that it is going to be that way— *I'm going to feel real healthy, now I'm sick. Now I'm happy, now I'm sad. Now everybody is behaving themselves, now they're going nuts!*— we realize that's what we are a part of. I am part of this particular universe. On the last page of the Steps portion of the Twelve and Twelve, the second to last paragraph starts, and whenever I hear it, I have a little sadness. It says, "These little studies of our A.A's Twelve Steps now come to a close." I just can see Bill writing that. I think it probably made him feel real good. *These little studies,* which are what the whole book was, *now come to a close.* What do we do here when they come to a close? We start all over again with Rob or Sally—whoever is the next person we can carry the message to.

It comes to a close and it starts again. We have step one, and then we have step two. We experience the wonderful spiritual journey of our Twelve Steps over and over and over again. We experience it over and over again every time we sponsor somebody. We watch a hopeless wreck become a hopeful and halfway there become a very useful AA member sponsoring three people, making the coffee, attending the intergroup functions.

Wow. Then, we meet a brand-new person. *Oh, you're a mess. I don't even think God can help you.* Then He does, and I go, *God, I never thought he could have possibly made it. That's beyond my wildest dreams. I can't believe that guy is sitting over there, totally responsible. Absolutely incredible.*

Our stories are coming to a close. It's just been delightful, but I'm leaving a loose end that I haven't talked about. This is just my take on it. We punctured the shell and saw the light. We're entering something that we really don't understand, which is God and the universe. How do we communicate and relate to this discovery?

We know that our thinking does nothing but screw things up. Thinking would be the worst possible way to do this. What's left? Well, I'll tell you something that I came across about a year ago in a history book. When Bill was getting near his old age, he wrote a letter to a friend reflecting on how he saw AA at that time.

This is what he called AA. He said that it was "an utter simplicity which encases a complete mystery." In our Twelve Steps, there isn't anything simpler than those steps. It is a very simple program. Dr. Bob said, "Keep it simple." We take these very simple actions. The ego gets cracked, and we behold a complete mystery. That is what we are now trying to relate to. When I was thinking about it, I thought, *What if I was a composer of symphony music and I wrote a symphony? What if I wanted to know how you all felt about my symphony?*

Now, one way would be to wait for the end of the performance and see if everybody stood up and gave a standing ovation. But standing ovations are getting to be pretty perfunctory. At the end of *everything*, we stand up and applaud. We may not mean it, but we stand up and applaud. That's not very good. Something that might be better would be to be behind the curtain and have binoculars, so that you could look at the faces while the music was being played. I think you would get all the information you would need by just watching the audience: sadness, wonder, total rapture, totally lost in the music, totally consumed by the precise moment.

Now, that would be quite a message if you were the composer. Wouldn't that make the composer happier than anything you could ever say? Could you top that with any kind of words? You couldn't. Maybe as we step into this, we have to fully accept it's a complete mystery. We have to become mystery beholders instead of mystery sleuths. There's nothing to figure out. It is beyond figuring out. You simply don't know. We get happy with not knowing.

There's nothing to know. There's just a show to behold. The first question we're going to get when we get back over into the magic place is, *Did you enjoy the show? I absolutely told you to insist on enjoying life, to display enjoyment.* If I want a wonderful life and a wonderful universe and a wonderful God, maybe I should just look at the definition of these words: "full of wonder."

Full of wonder. It's that simple. There's nothing left to do but that. Isn't that amazing? Now, there was a great hero of mine who passed away about twenty years ago. Everybody knows him. He's our dear brother, Louis Armstrong. When I think of Louis Armstrong, this is what I think of:

I see trees of green, red roses too.
I see them bloom, for me and you.
And I think to myself,
What a wonderful world.

I see skies of blue, and clouds of white.
The bright blessed day, the dark sacred night.
And I think to myself,
What a wonderful world.

The colors of the rainbow, so pretty in the sky.
Are also on the faces, of people passing by.
I see friends shaking hands, sayin', "How do you do?"
They're really sayin', "I love you."

I hear babies cryin', I watch them grow.
They'll learn much more, than I'll ever know.
And I think to myself.
What a wonderful world.

Yes, I think to myself,
What a wonderful world.

Thank you, and good night.

Appendix

THE 12 STEPS OF ALCOHOLICS ANONYMOUS

1.   We admitted we were powerless over alcohol—that our lives had become unmanageable.

2.   Came to believe that a Power greater than ourselves could restore us to sanity.

3.   Made a decision to turn our will and our lives over to the care of God *as we understood Him.*

4.   Made a searching and fearless moral inventory of ourselves.

5.   Admitted to God, to ourselves, and to another human being the exact nature of our wrongs.

6.   Were entirely ready to have God remove all these defects of character.

7.   Humbly asked Him to remove our shortcomings.

8.   Made a list of all persons we had harmed, and became willing to make amends to them all.

9.   Made direct amends to such people wherever possible, except when to do so would injure them or others.

10.   Continued to take personal inventory and when we were wrong promptly admitted it.

11.   Sought through prayer and meditation to improve our conscious contact with God, *as we understood Him*, praying only for knowledge of His will for us and the power to carry that out.

12.   Having had a spiritual awakening as the result of these Steps, we tried to carry this message to alcoholics, and to practice these principles in all our affairs.

THE 12 TRADITIONS

(SHORT FORM)

1. Our common welfare should come first; personal recovery depends upon A.A. unity.

2. For our group purpose there is but one ultimate authority—a loving God as He may express Himself in our group conscience. Our leaders are but trusted servants; they do not govern.

3. The only requirement for A.A membership is a desire to stop drinking.

4. Each group should be autonomous except in matters affecting other groups or A.A. as a whole.

5. Each group has but one primary purpose—to carry its message to the alcoholic who still suffers.

6. An A.A. group ought never endorse, finance, or lend the A.A. name to any related facility or outside enterprise, lest problems of money, property, and prestige divert us from our primary purpose.

7. Every A.A. group ought to be fully self-supporting, declining outside contributions.

8. Alcoholics Anonymous should remain forever nonprofessional, but our service centers may employ special workers.

9. A.A., as such, ought never be organized; but we may create service boards or committees directly responsible to those they serve.

10. Alcoholics Anonymous has no opinion on outside issues; hence the A.A. name ought never be drawn into public controversy.

11. Our public relations policy is based on attraction rather than promotion; we need always maintain personal anonymity at the level of press, radio, and films.

12. Anonymity is the spiritual foundation of all our Traditions, ever reminding us to place principles before personalities.

THE 12 CONCEPTS FOR WORLD SERVICE

(SHORT FORM)

The Twelve Concepts for World Service were written by A.A.'s co-founder Bill W., and were adopted by the General Service Conference of Alcoholics Anonymous in 1962.

The Concepts are an interpretation of A.A.'s world service structure as it emerged through A.A.'s early history and experience. The short form of the Concepts reads:

1. Final responsibility and ultimate authority for A.A. world services should always reside in the collective conscience of our whole Fellowship.

2. The General Service Conference of A.A. has become, for nearly every practical purpose, the active voice and the effective conscience of our whole society in its world affairs.

3. To insure effective leadership, we should endow each element of A.A.—the Conference, the General Service Board and its service corporations, staffs, committees, and executives—with a traditional "Right of Decision."

4. At all responsible levels, we ought to maintain a traditional "Right of Participation," allowing a voting representation in reasonable proportion to the responsibility that each must discharge.

5. Throughout our structure, a traditional "Right of Appeal" ought to prevail, so that minority opinion will be heard and personal grievances receive careful consideration.

6. The Conference recognizes that the chief initiative and active responsibility in most world service matters should be exercised by the trustee members of the Conference acting as the General Service Board.

7. The Charter and Bylaws of the General Service Board are legal instruments, empowering the trustees to manage and conduct world service affairs. The Conference Charter is not a legal document; it relies upon tradition and the A.A. purse for final effectiveness.

8. The trustees are the principal planners and administrators of over-all policy and finance. They have custodial oversight of the separately incorporated and constantly active services, exercising this through their ability to elect all the directors of these entities.

9. Good service leadership at all levels is indispensable for our future functioning and safety. Primary world service leadership, once exercised by the founders, must necessarily be assumed by the trustees.

10. Every service responsibility should be matched by an equal service authority, with the scope of such authority well defined.

11. The trustees should always have the best possible committees, corporate service directors, executives, staffs, and consultants. Composition, qualifications, induction procedures, and rights and duties will always be matters of serious concern.

12. The Conference shall observe the spirit of A.A. tradition, taking care that it never becomes the seat of perilous wealth or power; that sufficient operating funds and reserve be its prudent financial principle; that it place none of its members in a position of unqualified authority over others; that it reach all important decisions by discussion, vote, and whenever possible, substantial unanimity; that its actions never be personally punitive nor an incitement to public controversy; that it never perform acts of government; that, like the Society it serves, it will always remain democratic in thought and action.

THE AA PROMISES

1. If we are painstaking about this phase of our development, we will be amazed before we are half way through.

2. We are going to know a new freedom and a new happiness.

3. We will not regret the past nor wish to shut the door on it.

4. We will comprehend the word serenity and we will know peace.

5. No matter how far down the scale we have gone, we will see how our experience can benefit others.

6. That feeling of uselessness and self-pity will disappear.

7. We will lose interest in selfish things and gain interest in our fellows.

8. Self-seeking will slip away.

9. Our whole attitude and outlook upon life will change.

10. Fear of people and of economic insecurity will leave us.

11. We will intuitively know how to handle situations which used to baffle us.

12. We will suddenly realize that God is doing for us what we could not do for ourselves

Are these extravagant promises? We think not. They are being fulfilled among us —sometimes quickly, sometimes slowly. They will always materialize if we work for them.

Reprinted from the Big Book of Alcoholics Anonymous pages 83, 84
Published by A.A. World Services, Inc.

Epilogue

RICHARD JOHN "SANDY" BEACH

Richard "Sandy" Beach, an Icon of Alcoholics Anonymous, Spread a Message of Hope to Thousands.

—*Andrew Meacham, Tampa Bay Times Times Staff Writer*

In Alcoholics Anonymous, everybody knows everybody on first-name basis. People in AA keep a low public profile, lest a fall from sobriety reflect badly on the program.

Popularity, however, has created exceptions to the rule. Most people know the last names of AA co-founders Bill W. and "Dr. Bob"–Wilson and Smith. On the speaking circuit, from small meetings to big conventions, certain names carry enough cachet that their anonymity fades away. And audiences play recordings of their talks the way others listen to a favorite album.

Thus tens of thousands of AA members knew that the last name of popular speaker Sandy B. was actually Beach. A good chunk might know that he lived in Florida or that he had been a fighter pilot in the Marines.

Mostly they knew his messages about developing a spiritual life beyond abstinence, about letting go of control and tapping into what he called "the magic" they had once sought through alcohol. They knew his self-deprecating humor, which made the often-tough rhetoric easier to swallow.

Mr. Beach, a retired lobbyist for credit unions whose tireless efforts on behalf of AA made him one of its most recognizable names, died Sunday during an AA meeting in Tampa. He was 83.

The man, who had described himself as shy, tried to cap his speaking engagements to 26 weeks a year but often exceeded that limit. In a quietly spellbinding way, interweaving AA history and his own, Mr. Beach always came back to the program's fundamentals as outlined in its literature: *Alcoholics Anonymous*, known as the Big Book, and *Twelve Steps and Twelve Traditions*, or the "12 & 12."

He believed emphatically in AA's 12 steps, especially the first one about admitting powerlessness over alcohol.

"The point of the first step, quite frankly, is to convince you that your situation is a lot worse than you think it is," he said in 1994 talk. Consequently, it is the only step "you have to take 100 percent."

" 'Almost' doesn't cut it. Almost getting sober is very much like almost having a parachute after the plane gets blown up and you're up in the air."

Richard John Beach was born in New Haven, Conn., in 1931, the son of an engineer. He had his first drink at a college mixer, where he found alcohol made him feel more sociable. After graduating from Yale University, he joined the Marine Corps. His assignments included Florida, Virginia and Japan, and he taught pilots the bruising art of landing on aircraft carriers.

Mr. Beach spent close to a decade in the Marines, leaving as a captain, his family said. He stopped drinking Dec. 7, 1964 (Pearl Harbor Day, he reminded audiences). He lived in the Washington, D.C., area and worked for the Credit Union National Association.

His marriage to Barbara Platt, with whom he raised six children, lasted 17 years.

His activism in AA increased over time. At a 1976 convention in Palm Desert, Calif., to uproarious laughter, Mr. Beach compared his lifestyle with trying to swim while carrying a heavy rock.

His "Drop the Rock" talk, still famous in AA circles, launched a parallel unpaid career as a sought-after speaker.

"He could take the most complex thoughts you could come up with and distill it in simple terms," said Chris B., 53, of Tampa, whose last name is withheld to protect his anonymity, as with other AA members who were interviewed.

Mr. Beach went on to speak at international AA conventions and in several European countries.

He retired to a Bayshore Boulevard condominium in 1995, and stayed in shape by running up and down its 20 floors five times before bed.

Mr. Beach sponsored other men in AA who relied on him for steady guidance.

"There were times when the Marine came out, the salty language," said Dick C., a 63-year-old developer who was mentored by Mr. Beach. "He'd say, 'What part of the blankety-blank do you not blankety-blank understand'

"Then he'd sit back and smile. He wasn't mad. He was just getting your attention."

Recent Years included challenges, both emotional and physical. In 2010, daughter Barbara Hamburg, 48, was found bludgeoned to death outside her Madison, Conn., home. Another daughter, Catherine Barrett, 52, died three months later of liver disease, Mr. Beach's family said.

Mr. Beach also suffered chronic pain and congestive heart failure. He used a walker, then a wheelchair. He fell in September and spent weeks in the hospital.

Another AA member, Randy M., drove Mr. Beach to a 7.30 p.m. meeting Sunday at Palma Ceia Presbyterian Church. Mr. Beach had started the step study and speaker meeting a decade or so ago. As the meeting stated, Randy, 54, fetched Mr. Beach a cup of black coffee. Group members read AA's Preamble, which spells out the program's mission and its steps, then took turns reading from the 12 & 12.

"I asked him if he was okay," Randy said. "He looked at me and said, "Thanks for bringing me to the meeting, buddy."

Moments later, Randy said, he heard a slight gasp from Mr. Beach, whose head had slumped over on to the table. A member who is also a nurse rushed over to check his pulse. Another member, a physician, checked the carotid artery.

Mr. Beach was declared dead at the scene. His friends couldn't help but notice that he had died with his head on page 23 of the 12 & 12, from which the group had been reading.

The passage covers the first step.

First published in the Tampa Bay Times, Thursday, October 2, 2014

From the Publisher

HOTCHKISS PUBLISHING is founded on the simple belief, so well expressed by Nelson Mandela in his 1994 inaugural speech," that as we let our own light shine, we unconsciously give other people permission to do the same." We hope that the words and ideas expressed by our authors remove fears, give hope, provide guidance, and open doors thought to be closed. May they assist you during your journey through this life to discover the greatness which lies within you.

In the spirit of "full disclosure" I would like you to know that Sandy Beach was my first cousin. I am blessed to have grown up in the same small Connecticut town and to have known him all my life. I am immensely grateful for the support and wisdom he provided to me along my spiritual journey of the past 19 years. It is a privilege and a blessing to have the opportunity to keep his legacy and message of hope alive, in print, for all who loved him and for those yet to discover and benefit from his wisdom.

I would like to acknowledge and thank Allison Hagan for a terrific job editing the raw transcription from audio and developing it into a readable text. She went above and beyond to keep it flowing and faithful to Sandy's "voice". Thanks to my brother Rick Ludwig for his diligent copy edits and proofing the manuscript and his for advice and encouragement along the way.

It seems only fitting that this edition is being launched at the same time as the 80th Anniversary celebration of Alcoholics Anonymous in Atlanta Georgia.

I would like express my gratitude and love for Sandy's children Conway, Chris, Louis, and Richard. Thank you for allowing me to bring your father words to the printed page so that they will live on for future generations.

HOTCHKISS PUBLISHING welcomes your comments and ideas for future projects.

Please send them to: Bill@HotchkissPublishing.com

Milton Keynes UK
Ingram Content Group UK Ltd.
UKHW011318150324
439582UK00010B/846

9 780990 902010